The Story of Emily
~ a Proverbs 31 woman ~

Kress Christian
PUBLICATIONS

Diana Lynn Severance

Published by:
Kress Christian Publications
www.kressbiblical.com

Unless otherwise indicated, all scripture quotations are from the King James Version.

ISBN: 978-1-934952-31-3

Contents

Preface

Emily Augusta Severance lived most of her sixty years, from 1838 to 1898, in Vermont. Beginning her life in the youthful years of the American republic, Emily saw and experienced the grief and anguish of the Civil War. She became a pastor's wife and ably helped her husband encourage the church members in their Christian walk. With a love of learning, Emily early became a writer of poetry and other works, some of which were published in magazines when she was yet a teenager. A skilled and dedicated teacher, she often boarded students in her home to prepare them for the university, all the while raising five children of her own. She recognized that the upbringing of her children was the most important duty given to her, and she frequently prayed for wisdom and discretion as she directed their paths - all these accomplishments while sewing all the clothes for the family, preparing the meals for the large family and many guests, and managing a 19th century household.

For over thirty years Emily kept a diary, though at times sporadically, as a spur to reflection and consecration of her life to the Lord's work. Through her diary we have a glimpse into Emily's soul, her thoughts, trials, prayers, and triumphs. Though her 19th century world differs greatly from ours, many of her spiritual concerns are similar and can offer us an example and encouragement in our own Christian walk.

Emily noted that she especially enjoyed reading biographies and memoirs: "They seem to me like introductions to persons whom I expect to know hereafter, and the more I can learn of them now the more will my interest in them be enhanced when I come to know them personally." May you enjoy meeting Emily Augusta, knowing she will be one of the saints with whom we can spend a glorious eternity with our Savior and King.

Prologue

"Which we have heard and known, and our fathers have told us.
That the generations to come might know them,
even the children which should be born,
that they may arise and declare them to their children,
That they may set their hope in God
and not forget the works of God
but keep His commandments." Psalm 78:3, 6-7

Though our story properly begins in the 1830's, we must look centuries earlier for its life-giving roots. In the 1630's they came by the thousands – middle class Englishmen leaving behind their lands and old lives to forge new lives in America. Some came as families; some came as singles and formed new families in the new land. Among the latter were five Spencer siblings from Bedfordshire, England.

The Bedfordshire Spencers were yeoman farmers connected with distinguished families in the region. Gerard Spencer, Sr. (1576 – c.1645) lived through a time of tremendous economic, political, and religious change. When he was 11, the Spanish Armada attempted its invasion of England. As he grew into manhood, he lived through the prosperous, stable reign of Queen Elizabeth and became aware of the growing influence of Reformation and Puritan thought in the affairs of the church. As their name signified, the Puritans wanted to "purify" the English church of non-biblical and un-biblical practices and teachings. The Puritans believed Christians could find guidance and direction for every area of life from the Scriptures. Mostly members of the growing English middle class, Puritans held positions of some stature in both business and Parliament. The Puritan influence was strong in Gerard Spencer's Bedfordshire. John Bunyan, preacher and author of *Pilgrim's Progress*, would come from Bedford.

King Charles I, as his father King James before him, had great disdain for the Puritans and thoroughly opposed the reforms they wanted. When the king dissolved Parliament in 1628, it became obvious that there was no longer a method for the Puritans to work within the government and bring about reforms in either church or state. It seemed Providential that in the same year the king agreed to the Massachusetts Bay Charter, allowing the Puritans to establish a government of their own across the sea in America.

While Gerard Spencer, Sr. remained in England and saw the beginning of the English Civil War, five of Gerard's eight children, William (1601-1640), Elizabeth (b. 1602), Thomas (1607-1687), Michael (1611-1653) and Gerard, Jr. (1614-1685), sought refuge in America, becoming part of what has been called the Great Migration to Massachusetts.[1] Between 1629 and 1640, over 20,000 men, women, and children left England to settle in the Massachusetts Bay Colony. This immigration was called "Great" not just because of the numbers involved, but because of the greatness of the immigrants' purpose, which was more spiritual than economic. Most of the immigrants were from the English middle class and were leaving behind a comfortable living in England for an unsettled wilderness. Yet, they chose to leave behind what they saw as a corrupt England for the opportunity to live in a commonwealth governed by the truth of Scriptures. As a

---

[1] Lynn Betlock, "New England's Great Migration," www.greatmigration.org.

group, they were highly literate, and many were skilled artisans and craftsmen.

The five Spencer siblings were all young and of an age for setting forth into a new land – William being 29, Elizabeth 28, Thomas 23, Michael 19, and Gerard, Jr. 16. That they all were Puritans in faith is evident by the fact that the four men were all admitted into Massachusetts as freemen and served in various capacities in the government of their towns or colony.

Some sources indicate older brother William had attended Trinity College, Cambridge, where Puritan influence was strong. Very possibly he was involved in the organization of the Massachusetts Colony, since he was part of the General Court from the earliest records of the Massachusetts Colony and described as a "principal gentleman" of the colony. William is noted as among eight who established Newtowne, later renamed Cambridge, Massachusetts, in the spring of 1631. Both William and Thomas Spencer are shown to have dwellings in Newtowne in 1635. Younger brothers Michael and Gerard probably stayed with their older brothers at first, though both had small land grants of four acres each by 1635. Sister Elizabeth married Tommie Tomlins and lived in Lynn, Massachusetts.

The pastor at Newtowne, Rev. Thomas Hooker, came to disagree with the Puritan leaders of Massachusetts, wanting a more congregational form of government in both church and state and favoring more tolerance towards other Christian groups. In 1636, he led his congregation southward and formed the colony of Connecticut.[2]

---

[2] Lucius Paige. *History of Cambridge, Massachusetts, 1630-1877 with a Genealogical Register.* Boston: H.O. Houghton & Co., 1877,xvi-xvii, 8, 11, 17, 21, 32-33, 36, 42-43, 397, 460, 463, 468, 659.

William and his brother Thomas followed Hooker to Hartford in 1639.[3] The Fundamental Orders of Connecticut had been adopted in January of that year. Some speculate that William's quick acceptance into a position of leadership in the new Connecticut colony suggests he had been closely associated with Hooker in Cambridge. In 1639, William became a selectman of Hartford and a deputy of the general court of Connecticut.

The younger Spencer brothers, Michael and Gerard, moved to Lynn, Massachusetts, where more land was available. The constant movement westward was characteristic of this colonial society. Massachusetts Bay and the other New England colonies were organized into townships. It was most advantageous to be a proprietor in a town when it was first organized. Proprietors obtained the largest land grants and rights to share in future divisions of lands, a right important to their future heirs. Towns limited the number of proprietors, so that a town was considered closed once the number had been reached. New towns were continually being organized on the expanding frontier, providing land for the immigrants' children and grandchildren.

Elizabeth Spencer and her husband Timothy Tomlins had been leaders at Lynn since the early days of the settlement. Lynn was settled by 5 families who emigrated from Salem in 1629. Elizabeth and Timothy had come in 1630. In 1639 the General Court of Massachusetts granted Gerard Spencer "the ferry at Linn, for two years, taking 2^d for a single person to the furthest place, and but a 1^d for a person for more, to the furthest place, and but a 1^d for a single person to the nearest place."[4]

---

[3] William and Thomas are listed among the founders of Hartford, Connecticut: www.FoundersofHartford.org .

[4] Alonzo Lewis and James R. Newhall. *History of Lynn*, 183.

Before moving to Lynn, Gerard had married Hannah Hill.[5] Thirteen children were born to the couple. Gerard and his family lived in Lynn for twenty years, acquiring extensive amounts of land – woodland, pastureland, and swamp, as well as cultivatable land. About 1660, Gerard moved his family to Hartford, Connecticut, where his older brothers William and Thomas had been founding settlers. Gerard had been buying land in Hartford, as well as Haddam, before his move there.

In 1661, an interesting court case arose over whom Gerard's daughter Hannah would marry: *Simon Lobdell vs. Hannah and Gerard Spencer.* At issue: "She for refusing to marry with him according to promise and he for breach of promise." Though Simon Lobdell had sued for £150, the Court granted him only £15 and costs. Two years later Hannah married Daniel Brainerd. The couple had eight children, including Hezekiah, who was the father of the famous missionary to the Indians, David Brainerd.

Gerard stayed in Hartford for only a few years. Possibly he was waiting for the General Court to open up land south of Hartford, where his children would have better prospects to establish their families. In 1662, the land transaction was completed for the purchase of one hundred thousand acres from "four Indian Kings and two Indian Queens." Gerard Spencer, his son John, Daniel Brained, and twenty-four other men began the settlement that became Haddam, Connecticut. Gerard became the patriarch of the town, living there until his death in 1685, with many of his sons and daughters establishing leading families of the town. As part of

---

[5]For details on Gerard Spencer's life see Jack T. Spencer and Edith W. Spencer, "A Pioneer of Cambridge: Gerard Spencer," *The Connecticut Nutmegger*, March 1997, 592-613.

Gerard's will, he left "a pewter flagon and a rim basin to ye Church at Haddam, if there be one within five years." [6]

During his long life, Gerard Spencer consistently served his community in various capacities. He was captain of the train band or militia and member of the General Court of Connecticut 1674, 1679, 1680, and 1683. Even when in his sixties he is listed as an Ensign in King Philip's War. Given his long life and his extensive land holdings, Gerard was undoubtedly the wealthiest of the five immigrant Spencer siblings and the wealthiest man in Haddam at the time of his death. Having thirteen living children was an asset, giving him a large labor pool. That so many lived to adulthood was unusual during that period. Gerard's will left detailed bequests to his children and grandchildren. His youngest son Nathaniel (1658 - c.1752) received a dwelling and a lot, and a "30 pound right" to property on the east side of the river.

Nathaniel married Lydia Smith, and the couple remained in Haddam all of their lives, raising nine children in the growing community along the Connecticut River. Most of the tillable land in Haddam was located along the river, which provided an important source of income and transportation. Fishing, timber, and granite provided revenue. Shipyards were built along the river, and the many tributaries provided waterpower for mills. By 1720, Haddam had a population of 500. New generations would have to move inland to find fertile land.

Nathaniel, Jr. (1684-1767) married Hannah, and had nine children, whom they raised in Haddam. Early schools in Haddam had been in private homes and in one room school houses erected throughout the district. In 1750, the first record of district schools was kept, and Nathaniel Spencer, along with John Ventres and

---

[6] Jack Taif Spencer and Edith Woolley Spencer. *The Spencers of the Great Migration, Vol. 1, 1300-1783 A.D.*, Baltimore, Maryland: Gateway Pres, Inc., 1997, 229.

Thomas Brooks, was chosen for the school board.[7] Hannah died in 1741, and after two years, Nathaniel married Elizabeth Lee, by whom he had nine more children! In 1761, Nathaniel moved to Spencertown, New York and then sold his property in Haddam, where his family had lived for one hundred years.

In 1762, after Nathaniel Spencer, Jr. had moved from Haddam to New York, Nathaniel III (1723-1809), the seventh child of Nathaniel and Hannah Spencer, sold the Haddam property he had from his father and moved to New Haven, Connecticut. There he married Abigail English. The couple had eight children, the oldest being Jabez, born March 18, 1764. Jabez' name was given to him in honor of a relative of that name: "A hopeful young man who signalized himself in the late Action at Lake George; and returning home was killed by the breaking of his gun on the road, within three or four miles of his father's house, 1754."[8]

Jabez was a child when the American Revolution began, but he would have strong memories of the war. He was nine years old when the British under General William Tryon raided New Haven in July 1779. Though the British occupied the town only a week, the violence was unforgettable. Jabez' grandfather, Benjamin English, met a horrific death during the occupation, stabbed in his own home by British soldiers. As later recorded in the state records:

> Abigail English wife [Abigail was actually the daughter, not wife] of Capt. Benjamin English of New Haven of lawful age testifies and says that on the 5th day of July when the Brittish troops came to New Haven, Mr. Benjamin English aged about seventy four years was in his house alone. She saw a number of the Brittish troops at his well drinking water, that soon after she

---

[7] "History of Haddam," on the Haddam Historical Society website, http://www.haddamhistory.org/history_haddam.htm .
[8] From Jean Perry's "Golden Wedding Book" on the Spencer family.

saw a soldier come out at the back door, said English came to
the back door with his hands on his breast and the blood
running and he crying out, He has stabb'd me he has stabb'd
me. She asked him why he stab'd him. He answer'd, he could
not tell, for he had humour'd them as much as lay in his power,
and he walked about two rods and fell down and instantly
expired there appeared three wounds in his breast as if made
with a bayonet, that she went into the house found blood in the
great chair where he was wont to sit where she has the utmost
reason to suppose he receiv'd his mortal wound.

New Haven, July 28, 1779

Mrs. Abigail English the above deponent made solemn oath to
the above deposition.[9]

Though only 17 at the time of Yorktown, the last major battle of
the War, Jabez did serve as a private at some point during the war,
though in what engagement or alarm is not now known.[10]

Jabez married Joanna Ives on June 28, 1786, in New Haven,
Connecticut. They had three children in New Haven: Amelia,
Joseph Ives, and Nathaniel. Nathaniel (1792-1879) would become
the father of Emily Augusta, the focus of our story. Jabez and his
family left New Haven, living first in Mt. Holly, Vermont, and
then in Stockbridge. In 1807, Jabez settled his family on Otter
Creek, in Salisbury, Vermont.[11] The area especially began
attracting settlers after the American Revolution, but the
Revolutionary heritage of western Vermont remained strong in
those post-war years.

[9] Charles J. Hoadly. *The Public records of the State of Connecticut, 1778-1780*,
Vol. 2. Hartford: The Case, Lockwood and Brainard Company, 1895, 550.
[10] DAR ancestry number A106934. Jabez' grave in Salisbury, VT is marked as
that of a Revolutionary soldier.
[11] H.P. Smith, ed. *History of Addison County, Vermont*. Syracuse, NY: D.
Mason & Co., Pubs., 608.

Prologue

Vermont's name came from the Green Mountains running the length of the state - *les Vert Monts* in French. Samuel Champlain had given this name to the mountains in 1609, when he explored the region around Lake Champlain, which bears his name. In 1666, the French built Fort St. Anne on Lake Champlain as protection from the Mohawks. In 1724, the British established the first permanent European settlement in Vermont when they built Fort Dummer in what is now southeastern Vermont. From 1689 to 1763, the French and British fought four colonial wars in part over who would control the vast lands of North America.

Conflicting English charters led to the colonies of New York, Massachusetts, and New Hampshire all claiming parts of the land of Vermont. New Hampshire was especially aggressive in its expansion into the region. From 1749 to 1764, New Hampshire Governor Benning Wentworth issued a series of 135 land grants between the Connecticut River and Lake Champlain. The grant for the town of Salisbury, chartered in 1761, was among these New Hampshire Grants. In 1764, at the end of the French and Indian War, King George III of England drew a firm boundary between New Hampshire and New York. According to this new boundary, the lands of the New Hampshire Grants became part of the state of New York. When New York would not recognize the New Hampshire Grants, a strong opposition movement developed for a separate state. In 1770, Ethan Allen was chosen to lead the defense of the New Hampshire Grants in the New York (British) Courts, but lost the case.

When Ethan Allen returned to Vermont, he, along with his brothers Ira and Levi and his cousin Seth Warner, met with settlers at the Catamount Tavern in Bennington to decide on their next course of action. It was there that the Green Mountain Boys was organized to protect Vermonters from the New York authorities. In March 1775, a New York judge arrived at the courthouse in Westminster to enforce New York's control over the territory. He found the courthouse controlled by citizens intent on maintaining the New Hampshire Grants. The judge called for the sheriff to bring order to the protestors. In the end, two young Vermonters, Daniel Houghton and William French, were killed in the struggle. Occurring one month before the shots fired at Lexington, some have considered this "Westminster Massacre" as the first battle of the American Revolution.

The ranks of the Green Mountain Boys swelled after the events at Westminster, and Ethan Allen and others made calls for Vermont's independence. Two months later, on May 10, 1775, Allen and the Green Mountain Boys captured Fort Ticonderoga on Lake Champlain from the British. Ticonderoga's cannons captured by the Americans were later brought down to Boston by John Knox to end the British siege of Boston. Six months after American independence from Britain was declared in Philadelphia, Vermont declared itself an independent state. On July 8, 1777, the Constitution of Vermont was adopted. It was the first constitution in North America to provide for the abolition of slavery, give suffrage to men who did not hold property, and establish public schools.

Though the town of Salisbury was chartered in 1761, it was not truly established until after the American Revolution. During the war, the few families who first built homes there moved south to escape the forces moving down from Canada and attacking the colonists. By the time Jabez and his family arrived in Salisbury in 1807, numerous families had established farms in the rich farmland along Otter Creek. A school had been organized in 1789. Religious worship was begun in 1784, with the Congregational Church officially organized in 1804. A regular minister was called to the church in 1811. By 1810, Salisbury had a population of 709.

Nathaniel Spencer was 15 when he and his brother Joseph and sister Amelia came to Salisbury with their parents in 1807. He was at the right age to become a major contributor to building the house and cultivating the family farm in Salisbury. Families in Salisbury grew their own produce and found extra income through dairying and sheep as well as the abundant timbers still on the land. In 1821, when he was 29, Nathaniel became a member of the Congregational Church and continued faithful in attendance for over fifty years. Several of those years he served as deacon in the church.

In the early 1800s, through the end of the Civil War, Merino sheep became an important money-producer for the farmers. Luther Brown, an American Revolutionary soldier and early settler in Orwell, Vermont, was among the first to bring Merino sheep into western Vermont. In 1830, Nathaniel Spencer married Luther's daughter Esther. The couple settled in Salisbury, where Esther also became a member of the Congregational Church. Nathaniel continued work on the farm and was active in the community as well as the church. He was town clerk for twelve years and for several years served as Justice of the Peace.[12] When Salisbury formed a Gentlemen and Ladies' Auxiliary of the A.B.C.F.M. (American Board of Commissioners of Foreign Missions), Nathaniel was chosen Vice President.[13] He was also a supporter of the American Education Society, a homeland ministry of the Congregational Church to support schools and education for indigent youth.[14]

Nathaniel and Esther had seven children. Two children died at birth and one at the age of four. Four children lived to adulthood: Joseph Allen (b. 1834), Orrin Leroy (b. 1836), Emily Augusta (b.

---

[12]*Journal of the House of Representatives for the State of Vermont, 1936, 1938, 1939*; Leonard Deming. *Catalogue of the Principal Officers of Vermont.* Middlebury, 1851, 19.
[13] *Missionary Herald at Home and Abroad*, vol. 27-28, April 1831, 134.
[14] *Quarterly Register and Journal of the American Education Society*, 1839, 1840.

March 24, 1838) and Nathaniel (b. 1841). What follows is Emily Augusta's story.

Chapter 1 – The Foundation Laid

"Teach me thy way, O Lord, I will walk in thy truth: unite my heart to fear thy name." ~ Psalm 86:11

Emily Spencer's Salisbury lay in the shadows of the Green Mountains of Vermont. Sometimes obscured by mist and fog, the mountain peaks at other times gloried in the golden sunshine. The ever-shifting shadows moving over the mountains' sides focused the imagination on the power and strength of the Creator who had formed the hills. Wildflowers grew in the crevices of the huge mountain rocks, while alder and wild cranberry grew along the banks of Otter Creek below. In early spring, anemones showed their faces among the late snow. In summer, the meadows were full of lilies and wild strawberries. In August, blackberries were ripe for picking. The forests of maple produced maple syrup, while the hemlocks and pines provided lumber and firewood. Besides an abundance of trout, Otter Creek provided easy transport for lumber, wool, and other produce to markets at Lake Champlain and beyond.

As in all New England, and indeed much of the world, life in Salisbury was shaped by the seasons. Once the winter snows melted, the ground was ploughed and harrowed to prepare for sowing and planting. Each family had its own vegetable plots, and corn and potatoes were major crops. Hay from the meadows was continuously cut through August, providing winter fodder for the cattle. In the fall, vegetables were stored. Cider apples were taken to the mill; fall apples were dried for sauces. Paring bees were held to prepare apples for making apple sauce. Cords of wood were cut, and the house was prepared for the winter cold.[15]

Emily Augusta was born in Salisbury on March 24, 1838. She joined four-year-old Joseph Allen and two-year old Orrin Leroy as the children of Nathaniel and Esther Spencer. Brother Nathaniel would be born three years later.[16] As she grew, Emily learned the womanly skills and responsibilities needed on the Vermont farm. Women were particularly responsible for the cooking, clothing, and dairy. The women on the farm not only took care of the needs of their own family, but cooked and washed the clothing for any hired hands helping on the farm. The milking of cows and making butter and cheese were among the woman's sphere. Tallow candles were made from the fat of beef or sheep, with the wicking bought at the store. The women spun the thread and wove the cloth and then sewed the clothes for the entire family. Emily, as all young girls, early learned to sort wool, card it into rolls and work the spinning wheel. Cloth was woven for coverlets, tablecloths, towels,

---

[15] Descriptions of Salisbury, its seasonal life, and the particular training for girls during this period is taken from Mary Catherine Winchester's *Recollections of a Long Life, an Autobiography*, 6-101. The typescript of this memoir is in the Sheldon Museum of Middlebury, Vermont. Mary Catherine Severance Winchester became Emily's sister-in-law. She was ten years older than Emily and grew up near Middlebury, not far from Salisbury. Their young lives would have followed a similar pattern. A detailed description of the history and way of life in 18th century Salisbury can be found in John M. Weeks. *History of Salisbury, Vermont*. Middlebury, Vt.: A.H. Copeland, 1860. Emily Severance was a contributor to this local history.

[16] Two other children were born to Nathaniel and Esther Spencer before Emily's birth: Martha Spencer died the day of her birth in 1831; Luther was born 1832, but died in 1837. When Emily was two, Jane was born in 1840, but died the day of birth.

and clothes. Carpets were woven out of rags. Scraps of cloth were made into colorful quilts, whose patterns were given imaginative names such as rising sun, duck's foot in the mud, wild goose chase, and blazing star. In the summer, clothes were washed in the brook; in the winter, they were washed in melted snow.

Winters were cold, with snow often blowing down the chimney. Winter evenings were long, but became times of telling stories of the Indians and the Revolutionary War. The family regularly read the Bible together, and its words permeated the soul and language of Emily and the other Spencer children. Winter also became the time of formal schooling. A teacher boarded around in various homes for three months and provided some formal instruction to the young people of the community. Often the teachers were students from nearby Middlebury College.

When she was 13, Emily left home to attend school in Middlebury and then at the Seminary in Brandon, about 11 miles south of Salisbury. Though it was still unusual for girls to have more than a common school education, in the early nineteenth century there was a growing recognition that women needed to be educated in order to properly educate their own children The particular nature of the American government, resting on citizen participation, necessitated an educated and moral citizenry. Such education began at home, mostly under the mother's guidance and influence. Middlebury had been a leader in female education from the earliest days of its settlement. In 1800, when Middlebury College was founded, plans were also made to establish a female academy, which was formed the following year. One of the early teachers at the Middlebury Female Seminary was Emma Hart Willard, whose *Plan for Improving Female Education*, published in 1819, called for women to receive an advanced curriculum in the sciences and the classics similar to that offered in the men's colleges. At both Middlebury and Brandon, Emily received a classical education. She became proficient in Latin and took a delight in reading and literature.

The Congregational church in Salisbury was an important part of the life of the Spencers, as every Sabbath without fail the family went the four miles to the church, built in 1839, a year after Emily was born. Each Sabbath, the family would start for church at 10 o'clock, and reach home at three, after attending two services and the Sabbath school sandwiched in between. Rev. George Barrows was ordained and settled in Salisbury in 1845, when Emily was 7, and continued as pastor throughout her years in Salisbury. Friends described Rev. Barrows as "a man of firmness and decision, sweetness and evenness of temper, good sense, and perfection of character. His sermons were terse, forceful, and sound."[17] When she was 16, in 1854, Emily was admitted into membership of the Salisbury Congregational Church.

Emily undoubtedly on occasion attended Salisbury's Methodist Church, where Grandmother Joanna Spencer and some of her family were members. The Methodist church had a strong Sabbath School and held large Bible classes in the summer. The church library of 325 volumes testified to the congregation's focus on Christian education.[18]

As Emily left childhood behind and began to blossom into womanhood, she seriously considered her future, writing the following poem when she was fifteen:

What I Would Be
I would be young – but not for charm
Of joys which years can chase,
Not for the witching spells that lie

[17] *Minutes of the General Association of the Congregational Churches and Ministers of New York.* Education Society of the State of New York, 1881, 41.
[18] John M. Weeks. *History of Salisbury, Vermont.* Middlebury, Vermont, 1860, 188, 193.

In beauteous form and face;
But for the winning childlike trust,
 The ardent love of truth,
The innocence which brightest shines
 Upon the brow of youth.

I would be talented – but seek
 In earnest, humble way
To woo the smiles, where linger tears
 And send the grief away,
And if the tribute of the poor
 "God bless her," they should raise,
I'd prize that one petition more
 Than gathering earthly praise.

I would be eloquent – but oh!
 That thrilling power I'd use
To right the wrongs of suffering ones
 And hidden light diffuse,
I'd raise the voice of eloquence
 To crush oppression low,
To dig the grave of vice and crime
 And soothe the touch of woe.

I would be great – but not for fame
 Which liveth but a day
And while we list, its flattering speech
 Is vanishing away;
I would be great to raise the weak
 And cheer the broken heart;
To drop the tear of sympathy,
 And heal the affliction's smart.

I would be rich – but not for friends
    To vanish with my gold,
But for the power to feed the poor
    And sinking hands uphold.
I would be rich to bring to light
    The hidden gems of earth,
Which warmed by friendship's genial glow
    Would prove a priceless worth.

I would be loved – but not for wealth,
    Or beauty's winning smile,
For these can wake no answering chord
    Within my heart the while.
I would be loved for spirit pure,
    For loveliness of soul,
For o'er these charms the coming years
    Can never have control.

I would be good – oh, yes, and then
    The earth would all be bright,
And life would be one pleasant dream
    Of pure unmixed delight:
And when the summons come "Depart,
    For this is not your rest,"
I'd lay me gently down to sleep
    And wake among the blest.[19]

---

[19] Quoted in Emily Augusta's obituary in *The Middlebury Register* of June 17, 1898, clippings in "Day Papers," a collection of newspaper clippings in the Bennington Genealogical Society.

Friends later remembered that during this time Emily published other poems in local periodicals under the pseudonym "Linda Lee," but this author has not been able to locate examples of those.

In 1856, when she was eighteen, Emily entered Mount Holyoke Female Seminary in South Hadley, Massachusetts, 150 miles from Salisbury. Mary Lyon (1797-1849), a leader in female education, had founded Mount Holyoke Female Seminary in 1837, making it the oldest college for women in the United States. As a young lady, Miss Lyon had been an eager student herself, with an endless thirst for knowledge. She saw no reason to restrict female education to basic reading, writing and domestic skills, but thought women were perfectly capable of learning the sciences, mathematics, and the classical subjects taught in the male colleges. She believed, however, that knowledge itself was not enough. Knowledge should be useful, and education must give attention to the heart as well as the mind. A Christian of firm convictions, Miss Lyon believed that the Christian faith included all categories of learning, and at Mount Holyoke she made certain that religious instruction was most important and foundational. Students were to be molded into the likeness of Christ and trained for His service. Building character was an important part of Mount Holyoke's education program. Mary Lyon and her teachers were involved in educating and training young women to be useful in their world as teachers, wives, and mothers, serving in all things as unto Christ.

Emily's education at Middlebury and Brandon Seminaries enabled her to pass the examinations for the first year's course at Mount Holyoke and enter directly into the middle class. Studies for the middle class included Latin (Cicero), philosophy, chemistry, natural philosophy, astronomy, botany, rhetoric, trigonometry, and evidences of Christianity.[20] Emily was invigorated not only by the challenging curriculum, but also by the many life-long friendships she made with young women from all over New England.

In her second or senior year, Emily studied Latin (Cicero again), geology, Paley's *Natural* Theology, mental philosophy, logic, moral philosophy, Butler's *Analogy*, and Milton's *Paradise Lost*.[21] For the rest of her life, Emily was known to be able to recite much of Milton's epic poem from memory. The intellectual standards were as high at Mount Holyoke as at any of the male colleges, and Emily thrived. The well-regulated life at the seminary balanced long hours of study with times for recreation and usefulness, as each student shared in the domestic responsibilities of the school, which was like a large family. Foundational to all was Bible study and prayer, with the high calling ever held before the students of becoming a woman known for her Christ-likeness.

Emily would keep in touch with many of her Mt. Holyoke classmates throughout her life. Before graduating, she wrote a "Parting Hymn of Senior Class at Holyoke Seminary 1858," to be sung to the tune of "Auld Lang Syne:"

> The parting sunlight gently rests
>> Upon the Mountain brow,
> While gathering shadows darkly glide
>> Along the vale below.
> And joy and sorrow varying thus
>> Our bosoms swell,
> As tremblingly we breathe today

---

[20] *Twentieth Annual Catalogue of the Mount Holyoke Female Seminary in South Hadley, Massachusetts, 1856-1857.* Northampton: Thomas Hale and Company, 1857, 12.
[21] *Twenty-first Annual Catalogue of the Mount Holyoke Female Seminary in South Hadley, Massachusetts, 1857-1858.* Northampton: Thomas Hale and Company, 1858, 12.

The Foundation Laid

Our last farewell.

We pause upon the final page
      Of our three volume book,
And turning o'er the backward leaves
      With fondly lingering look,
Above the graces of many a hope
      We drop the tear,
And smile o'er many a new-found joy
      Recorded here.

And mournfully and tenderly
      We breathe a gentle sigh,
As memory opes the sacred leaf
      Where sorrows treasures lie;
One loving heart is lost to us
      But found above,
And the angels number sings
      A Savior's love,

But as we close the parting lids
      Upon the year now flown,
A noble volume opens wide,
      And each must read alone.
Its sterner lessons must be met,
      As ne'er of yore,
Unguided now by gentle hands
      Forevermore.

But though in lone and distant paths
      Our wandering steps may roam,
With loving hearts we'll journey on
      To yonder heavenly home.

And there before the eternal throne,
  With rapture new,
We'll meet and all life's buried page
  With joy renew.[22]

Graduating from Mount Holyoke in 1858, Emily returned to her family at Salisbury. Invigorating though her two years at Mount Holyoke had been, Emily was exhausted by her studies, having completed the three year course in two years. Besides her family in Salisbury, Emily would also be returning to Salisbury Congregational Church, where Milton Leonard Severance had become a member at the age of seventeen, in 1847. The Severances had a farm in nearby East Middlebury, and there is some question as to why Milton would attend the Salisbury church apart from the rest of his family. Most likely, Milton taught in the common school in Salisbury and elected to join the church there. If so, Milton would have been Emily's teacher for a time as well as a fellow-worshipper in Salisbury. Milton worked on his father's farm until he reached 21 in 1851, then he attended Johnson Academy and Burr and Burton Seminary in Manchester, Vermont in preparation for attending Middlebury College. Milton earned money throughout his college preparatory and college years by teaching school and arranging freight shipments from the paper mill in Middlebury to paper warehouses in New York and other eastern towns.[23] He was able to graduate from Middlebury in 1859, at the age of twenty-nine, with $150 in his pocket after paying all of his bills. Education and the life of the church continued an

---

[22]This poem is "An extract from the Class Album of My Mother, Laura Root (Johnson) Richards, Mt. Holyoke Seminary,1858," Mt. Holyoke Archives.
[23] When Emily began keeping her journal in 1866, she used a ledger book. The first few pages were accounts of sales to paper warehouses, dating 1854, 1856, 1859, and 1860. These were undoubtedly Milton's and indicate a means of him earning funds to complete his schooling.

integral part of the lives of Milton and Emily after the two were married in Salisbury on August 16, 1859.[24] Emily was twenty-one.

Milton, like Emily, was from a long line of Puritans stretching back to the earliest English settlements in Massachusetts. John Alden and Priscilla Mullens were among his *Mayflower* ancestors. Ancestor Robert Hicks arrived in Plymouth on the *Fortune* the following year, in 1621. One ancestral line, the Leonards, established the early iron works in Saugus, Massachusetts. The Severances, as were the Spencers, were part of the Great Migration, arriving in 1634 and settling in Salisbury, Massachusetts. Each generation moved further westward in search of farmland for the growing families, but throughout the westward migrations, the Congregational Church remained central to the life of the new communities. Ancestor John Severance was among the early settlers in Deerfield, of the infamous Indian raid of 1704. One ancestor, Ebenezer, was killed in his cornfield by the natives. Milton's grandfather, Samuel Severance, was among the founders of Middlebury, Vermont. Grandmother Mary Kirby Severance as a little girl held the reins of the couriers' horses while her father Abraham Kirby and two of her brothers fought at the Battle of Bennington. Stories across the generations from the days of the colonial settlement and the Revolution were repeatedly told in the family circle.

Emily and Milton's first residence as newlyweds was in Ticonderoga, New York. Ticonderoga, located at the strategic connection between Lake George and Lake Champlain, had seen important action in the eighteenth century wars for empire between France and England, as well as in the American Revolution. During the 1850's it was a busy shipping port transporting goods

---

[24] Such a scenario of how Emily and Milton might have met is not without precedent. Milton's sister Mary Catherine met her future husband, Warren Winchester, when he was a student at Middlebury College and teaching in the common school she attended.

and people on Lake Champlain. In 1858, the town began plans for establishing a high school, Ticonderoga Academy, and Milton was chosen the Academy's first principal, serving from 1859-1860. It would be the first of several principalships he would hold throughout his varied career, and Emily helped with the teaching.

March 16, 1860, Emily's grandmother Joanna Spencer passed away in Salisbury at the age of 92. She had been a young woman at the time of the American Revolution. Her passing seemed the breaking of a link with America's youth; at the time of her death, the United States was careening towards Civil War. At this tumultuous time for the nation, Milton resigned his post at Ticonderoga and began his formal training for the Christian ministry at Union Theological Seminary in New York City, where Emily and Milton set up housekeeping.

With the election of Abraham Lincoln in 1860, several southern states seceded from the United States. In March 1861, Lincoln called for troops to put down the rebellion. The next month, war began with the shots fired at Fort Sumter. Emily's brother Orrin was among the first to answer Lincoln's call to serve and enlisted in the Vermont infantry in August.[25] That August Milton applied for a chaplaincy in a Vermont regiment. Though Salisbury's Pastor Barrows sent a supporting letter of recommendation, Milton's application was unsuccessful.[26] It was in the midst of these war-time preparations that Emily was expecting her first child. She returned home to Salisbury, where she gave birth to Claude Milton on November 3, 1861.

There are few records of Emily's thoughts and actions during these Civil War years. She undoubtedly followed closely the activities of her brothers in the Union army, both by letter and by newspaper reports. Orrin was in the 5th Vermont Infantry,

---

[25] *Vermont in the Civil War.* http://vermontcivilwar.org/units/rr/162.php.
[26] Erastus Fairbanks Index. Vermont State Archives, MSVTSP, v. 81, 89, 93.

Company F. Most of the fall and winter of 1861-1862, the 5th
Vermont spent at Camp Griffin near Langley, Virginia. It saw
heavy fighting during the Peninsula Campaign, suffering heavy
losses at Savage's Station on June 29, 1862. Emily's younger
brother Nathaniel enlisted in the 14th Vermont Infantry in October
1862. The regiment's first assignment was the defense of
Washington, D.C.

In 1862, Milton transferred to Andover Seminary for his final
year of seminary. Undoubtedly Emily felt more at home in the
New England town of Andover, Massachusetts than in the bustling
metropolis of New York. 1862-1863 was not only a time of both
intense sorrow and happiness for Emily, but it was a critical period
for the conduct of the Civil War.

Orrin's 5th Vermont regiment participated in the Maryland
Campaign before encamping near Fredericksburg for the winter of
1862-63. Orrin saw action in the bloody battles of Fredericksburg
and Chancellorsville. Both Orrin and Nathaniel saw action at
Gettysburg, the biggest battle every fought in North America.
Orrin's regiment served as pickets on the extreme left of the
Union. In April 1863, Nathaniel's regiment became part of the
First Corps and began its march to the North, which ended at
Gettysburg, where the regiment saw its first military action. The
march itself was a grueling one, with almost one third of the men
falling out, unable to bear the killing pace. Nathaniel's regiment
reached Gettysburg in time to participate in the second day of
fighting, effectively repelling A.P. Hill's attack on the left center.
On the third day, when Pickett led his massive charge of seventeen
thousand troops, the Fourteenth remained concealed on the ground
until Pickett's men were within sixty yards: "The men rose at
command and gave a staggering and unexpected volley in the face

of the charging columns."[27] In leading the repulse of Pickett's charge, the 14th Vermont had 19 killed in action; nine dying later of wounds received, and 74 wounded. Among those mortally wounded was Emily's brother, Corporal Nathaniel Spencer. Nathaniel was taken home to Salisbury. He died six weeks later, August 20, 1863. Neither he nor his family could know at the time that Nathaniel had been a part of the important turning point in the war to save the Union.

Emily was with Nathaniel in Salisbury during his last days. Two days before her brother's death, on August 18, 1863, she was delivered of her second son, named Wilbert Nathaniel. As so often in life, moments of joy intermingled with times of grief.

Milton completed Seminary the spring of 1863. He then served as pulpit supply in Congregational churches. After he preached several times over the months in the pulpit of the Congregational Church in Boscawen, New Hampshire, the church members invited him to "become the pastor and teacher of this church and minister of this people" in September 1863.[28] Milton accepted the call and moved with Emily and his two boys to Boscawen.

Boscawen was then a pleasantly situated town on the western side of the Merrimack River with many excellent farms and abundant fruit trees. In the 1860s the population was about 2100. The town included an academy, sixteen common schools, two post offices, one cotton mill, one woolen factory, nine saw-mills, a grist-mill, a saw manufacturer and machine shop, a chair and match factory, five stores, and six houses of worship (2 Congregational, and one each of Baptist, Christian, Methodist, and

---

[27] Rev. William S. Smart. "14th Vermont Regimental History," *Revised Roster of Vermont Volunteers,* Montpelier, Vermont: Press of the Watchman Publishing Co., 1892, 502-523 as found at http://vermontcivilwar.org/units/14/history.php .
[28] Agnes Pillsbury. *The Story of Boscawen Church*. Concord, New Hampshire: W.B. Ranney Company, 1940, 44.

Union).[29] Milton was ordained and formally installed as pastor on Wednesday February 17, 1864, while the war continued to rage in Virginia.

In 1864, Orrin and the 5th Vermont Regiment took part in the terrible campaign from the Rapidan to Petersburg, with severe losses. In July, the regiment assisted in driving Jubal Early from Washington before becoming part of the Army of the Shenandoah. While settling into her first parsonage, Emily undoubtedly carefully read reports of these now historic engagements for any mention of Orrin or indications he was not among the killed or wounded. Orrin's enlistment was up in September 1864; he and most of his fellow soldiers chose not to re-enlist. Orrin mustered out with the rank of 1st Lieutenant.[30]

That fall Milton went out for a few weeks as a delegate with the United States Christian Commission. With the intense fighting of the Army of the Potomac in Virginia, the wounded increased in the Washington D.C. hospitals. Milton worked as a chaplain at Camp Distribution, the point of departure for those discharged from the hospitals, as well as convalescents and those being discharged as unfit for duty. The camp also housed stragglers, deserters, the recaptured, and new recruits awaiting to join their regiments. Conditions at the camp were poor, with nine or ten thousand men lodged in tents. Yet, in the middle of such dismal conditions, Milton and the other chaplains ministered the grace of Christ. Milton told of one soldier:

> The apostle says "By this shall ye know that ye have passed
> from death unto life, because ye love the brethren," and I have
> never seen a livelier test of this than a colored soldier gave at

---

[29] A.J. Coolidge and J.B. Mansfield. *A History and Description of New England, general and local, Vol. 1*. Boston: Austin J. Coolidge, 1859, 424-425.
[30] Hon. Lewis Addison Grant, John R. Lewis, and Charles G. Gould. *5th Vermont Infantry Regiment History from the 1892 Revised Roster*, www.Vermontcivilwar.org.

the close of one of our evening meetings. There was a simplicity in his expression and manner which touched all our hearts.

"I love my Saviour, I love the Church of Christ, I love the world, I love everybody, I love them that don't love me." I felt that the poor son of Africa had reached the climax of Christian experience. Like the martyred Stephen, and his Saviour before him, he could pray for those who had despitefully used him.[31]

Rev. William Winchester, husband of Milton's sister Mary Catherine and pastor in Clinton, Massachusetts, had enlisted as a military chaplain in June 1862, and was assigned to the Finley Hospital in Washington D.C. in 1863.[32] Once he had found a house for his family in Washington, William had Mary Catherine and the four children moved to the capital city. They were looking forward to expanding the horizons of the children and showing them the special sites of the city.

On their first Sabbath in Washington, the entire family attended church in the hospital tent, with William preaching and all the children singing hymns from the *Soldiers' Hymn Book*. William had sent the children a copy of the hymn book earlier, and the children were able to sing beautifully along with the rugged soldiers. Many of the soldiers gazed fondly at the children singing, wiping "the tears from their eyes, as they thought of their own little ones, at home, from whom this cruel war had separated them."[33] Tragically, within a week all the children were taken ill with diphtheria, and the three little girls, ages four through nine, died. Mary Catherine wrote Emily and Milton a moving description of

---

[31] Edward Parmelee Smith. *Incidents of the United States Christian Commission*. Philadelphia: J.B. Lippincott & Co., 1869, 373.
[32] http://vermontcivilwar.org/get.php?input=57227 Vermont in the Civil War Database
[33] Winchester. *Recollections of a Long Life*, 304.

the last days of the children, reflecting the childlike faith of the girls, who through their weakness and pain looked forward to being with Jesus.

The battles in Virginia filled the hospitals in Washington with the wounded and dying. Often Rev. Winchester heard the newly wounded brought from the battlefields across the bridge at night and arose to meet them. He wanted to gain as much information from the wounded as possible to share with their families, knowing that many would not survive until morning. Hopeful Scriptures of salvation and words of comfort for the Christian were a spiritual balm to the suffering soldiers. When the war ended, Winchester remained faithfully in Washington, until the last war hospital was closed. After the trial of the conspirators in Lincoln's assassination, the government appointed Winchester to visit with two of the conspirators, George Atzerodt and Lewis Powell, the day before their execution.[34] Winchester spent the night with them and walked to the scaffold with them in the morning.

Powell, the son of a Baptist minister in Florida, was a very athletic man. When Winchester asked him how he got involved in the conspiracy, he said he thought he was doing right. He had been taught the North was wrong about slavery, and he was trying to do his duty. Atzerodt was a much coarser fellow. He said when he joined Booth, he had no thought of killing the President, but thought Lincoln was going to be kidnapped and taken away somewhere. When he learned about the assassination plot, he told

---

[34] Atzerodt and Powell were two of the four conspirators executed on July 8, 1865. The night of Lincoln's assassination, Lewis Powell, who was tried under the name of Lewis Payne, the name he used when he signed the Oath of Allegiance at the conclusion of the war, attacked Secretary of State Seward and stabbed him and his two sons repeatedly. George Atzerodt was given the responsibility of killing Vice President Johnson, but was too cowardly to carry through the act and got drunk instead. Rev. Winchester was not assigned to visit Mary Surrat or David Herald, since they were Catholics and were assigned a Catholic chaplain.

Booth he was leaving him, but Booth pulled a pistol and said he would blow his brains out if he did. Atzerodt asked Winchester if he preached to the soldiers. When Winchester said he did, Atzerodt took his Bible and said, "I would give you this, but I have promised it to a friend." He tore out a flyleaf, however, and wrote down Luke 12:2,3,4 ("For there is nothing covered that will not be revealed, nor hidden that will not be known. Therefore, whatever you have spoken in the dark will be heard in the light, and what you have spoken in the ear in inner rooms will be proclaimed on the housetops.") He asked Winchester to preach the next Sabbath on those verses, which Winchester did.[35]

In the midst of national turmoil and upheavals, Emily enjoyed quiet peace in the parsonage at Boscawen, "the true idea of a home, full of love and comfort and cheer." She enjoyed the warm expressions of friendship from the congregation as the pastor and his people drew closer together. In the fall of 1865, Milton was severely ill for three months and unable to perform his duties. At the end of the year, when Emily wrote an entry for the Mount Holyoke class of '58, she began by noting, "My life has wound along in such a quiet, unobtrusive channel, that it hardly seems worth reporting, yet I remember that it is the little rills that feed the fountains." After recounting her move to Boscawen, Milton's illness, and the happiness of her two boys, she reflected:

> In the midst of duties and trials, the thing which impresses me most is my own weakness and insufficiency. How shall I gain an influence over the dear souls perishing around me? It matters little that others are climbing higher in intellectual endowments, but it humbles me when I think that I am left

---

[35] Winchester. *Recollections of a Long Life*, 335-336; Edward Steers, Jr. and Harold Holzer. *The Lincoln Assassination Conspirators, their confinement and execution as recorded in the letterbook of John Frederich Hartranft.* Baton Rouge: L.S.U. Press and Washington, D.C.: National Archives and Records Administration, 2009.

behind in spiritual growth. Is it not, my sisters, after all, the great desideratum to be able to dignify our lowly duties by the cheerful spirit which we bring to their performing, to have the testimony of a good conscience, and the smile of a benignant Father? I trust you will pray that I may have a new and more perfect baptism for my life work.[36]

This would be a recurrent thought and prayer throughout Emily's life. Recognizing that the daily affairs and encounters in a quiet life of being a wife and mother were to be consecrated to the Lord and bear fruit in ministering, Emily always sought a greater spiritual growth and productivity. To that end, as she approached her 28th birthday, Emily decided to begin a diary. She prefaced the work by noting,

Twenty-eight years have dug their trenches and laid their foundation and today this unfinished structure stands only at a beginning of the future. As an omen of that future it is fitting at such a time as this to come very near and examine the cornerstones whether they be laid in fair colors and descend into the trenches and ascertain whether they are wide enough and deep enough for the future edifice to rest upon.[37]

In keeping a diary, Emily was following a Puritan tradition of recording life's events as a way of recording God's work with an individual and the person's progress in Christian virtue. As Emily began her diary, she speculated that her outward life seemed full of business and goodness, but her intellectual life was full of indolence: "I suppose if my Lord should demand today the talent

---

[36] Emily Spencer Severance's letter in *Mount Holyoke Class of, '58 Letter,* 1859. Clipping of letter in back of Emily's journal.

[37] Emily Augusta Severance. *Diary,* March 24, 1866. Emily's *Diary* was given to the author by June and Spencer Severance. Spencer Severance was Emily and Milton's Severance's grandson and the brother of Gordon Barker Severance, also the grandson of Emily and Milton Severance as well as the author's husband. Quotes from Emily's journal will be cited by date.

which He gave me, I should have to go away in shame and drag
the unsightly carrion from the earth where I have laid it." Her diary
would become a spur to reflection and consecration of her life to
the Lord's work. Continued until the year before her death, the
thirty years of diary entries are a window into Emily's thoughts, as
well as a picture of the life of a pastor's wife, Christian mother,
and dedicated teacher in New England at the end of the nineteenth
century.

Chapter 2: A Home in Boscawen, New Hampshire

"be ye stedfast, unmoveable, always abounding in the work of the
Lord, forasmuch as ye know that your labour is not in vain."
~ I Corinthians 15:58

The philosophical introspection with which Emily prefaced her
journal was cut short by an unspecified "interruption." Her first
diary entry, March 26, 1866, two days after her twenty-eighth
birthday, noted, "I have been sick all day. I suppose I should never
forget it. MLS [Milton] has been my faithful attendant and
watched over me with more than a mother's tenderness."[38] Emily
continued in a weak condition for at least two weeks, but she never
gives the cause or full nature of her illness. She wrote about
enduring "intense suffering, pain, loss of strength, faintness, and
general exhaustion. For a little while I did not know but the
Beyond was very near me, but I was not un-reconciled to the
thought."[39]

---

[38] Quotes from Emily's journal will be cited by date. March 26, 1866
[39] March 28, 1866.

On the Sabbath, Emily stayed home with little Willie, reading the Bible and other books, but became so exhausted that she was in bed all afternoon with great pain. Emily notes in her journal that in the evening Milton and Carrie, the girl who helped in the house and kitchen, sang hymns

> breathing of Heaven and home. I asked myself if I was ready to die, and could only answer, I am unworthy to go into the presence of my God. I have always been unworthy, I shall always be unworthy, but Christ died for sinners, my only hope has always been and <u>now</u> is through Him. I trust His promises; I am not afraid to meet Him. Can you leave the dear children and the more solitary mourner? Yes, if it be God's will. He who taketh care for sparrows will not suffer His work to be hindered by my absence.[40]

In her illness, her submission to God's will was strengthened.

As Emily slowly recovered, she could do little work, but she could read! Reading the two volumes of William Cowper's life, she was moved by Cowper's love for friends and the deep melancholy of the poet's soul.[41] Never again could she read "There is a fountain filled with blood" without thinking of Cowper's hopeless years and the closer walk with God which he would enjoy.

As she regained her strength, Emily was able to return to her responsibilities at home and at church. She especially enjoyed hearing and meeting Rev. Lewis Grout, who spoke in Boscawen in April 1866. Grout had been a missionary among the Zulus for

---

[40] April 1, 1866. Emily's quotations or allusions to Scripture will be noted in the footnotes. I Corinthians 15:3; Matthew 10:29-31

[41] William Cowper (1731-1800) was an English poet, hymnodist and neighbor of the evangelical minister John Newton. He was often plagued by doubt and melancholy, but found refuge in his Christian faith. Cowper's most famous hymn: "There is a Fountain Filled with Blood."

fifteen years.[42] During that time he had so expended his energies in teaching agriculture, being a physician, studying the language and writing a grammar, translating the Bible, printing books, and preaching the gospel that he was forced to return to the United States for rest. He became secretary of the American Missionary Association for Vermont and New Hampshire. The American Missionary Association had been founded in 1846, shortly after the *Amistad* affair, as an anti-slavery missionary organization. After the Civil War, the American Missionary Association worked to further the education of the recently freed slaves. From his work among the Zulus, Grout knew first-hand that the African race had excellent reasoning powers, and he spoke convincingly about the importance of educating the freedmen in America. Emily found Grout a very pleasant man who gave her "some very interesting facts relative to animal and vegetable life in Africa, such luxuriant foliage, such beautiful birds, and such exquisite flowers, but oh the rainless months, the heat, the damp, the mould, the wild monsters of the forest, and the venomous serpents of the plain." Rev. Grout's parting words to little Claudie were, "Give your heart to the Savior and then it will be all right."[43] Would these encouraging words have any effect on the boy not quite five?

Rev. Grout spoke at the church meetings several times in following weeks, and Emily always found him inspiring. One evening he spoke on "the certainty of the fulfillment of God's purposes in bringing the whole world to himself." He compared God's plan to a wide river. Counter winds might strike the waves backward for a season, but underneath the river was always moving onward: "We see difficulties in the way, and at times are almost discouraged on account of this unbelief in our hearts and the determined assaults of the powers of darkness, but God's plans

---

[42] Hon. Hiram Carlton. *Genealogical and Family History of the State of Vermont,* vol. I, 193-198.
[43] May 13, 1866.

fail not."[44] Grout movingly told the difficulties of the missionary's task in a strange and hostile climate and not knowing the language. He explained in some detail the method of learning a spoken language from the people. After three months in Africa he was able to haltingly preach to the people; after eight years he could tolerably preach to the people; after fifteen he could preach as readily as in his own language.

Later in the summer, when Emily and Milton attended the New Hampshire Bible Society meeting in Concord, Emily heard Rev. William Butler, who had spent ten years in India. He explained the idolatry of the Hindus. When he exhibited one of the idols, Emily could only wonder, "Natural reason, unaided by revelation bows down to worship – what? – a monkey!"[45] The speakers on missions brought Emily's mind to her days at Mount Holyoke. Missions were powerfully presented there, and Emily had asked herself then if it wasn't her duty to go to the heathen with the gospel. She was ready whenever she had a clear call. Listening to Rev. Butler, she could imagine delightfully responding to such a call – but she knew it was not then her duty to carry Christ to the heathen. Her relations and surroundings precluded that. But did that mean she had nothing to do for Christ? –

> May it not be that God has given me a power for doing good which has been so long neglected that I am almost unconscious of it. Why not set myself in the thickest of the fight and seek to achieve victories at home as well as if I were [on] missionary ground in a foreign land? Then and there I made a second promise to myself, to be more thoroughly <u>alive</u>, more vigilantly awake, more zealously active in my Master's work. If I cannot be a missionary, I may be able to stimulate some hearts, now cold, with a mother's love, a deeper humility, a more

---

[44] May 13, 1866.
[45] June 19, 1866.

unswerving faith. I will at the very least show them that I for one am <u>in earnest</u>.[46]

As an encouragement to this calling, when Emily returned home she found a letter from a former pupil, Mary Delano. Emily had long been concerned for Mary's spiritual welfare, and she was joyful to read of the "dawn of religious truth in her soul." Her awakening was a triumphant case of the power of God. Mary had always been an intellectually moral person concerned about individual and social evils, but she wrote Emily that, "Morality was her greatest enemy, because she trusted in it and thought that was sufficient."[47] She now realized her sufficiency must be in Christ.

That spring Emily read a great abundance of books, and her journal became the repository for reflective reviews. She liked reading Miss Warner's religious novel *The Old Helmut*, though she didn't think the characters in the novel were realistic.[48] In every one of the books she introduced at least one man who was a paragon of perfection:

> I can only account for the fact on the consideration that she is not <u>married</u>. If she could witness for once the freaks of impatience and absurdity with which the best of men are frequently betrayed, at the loss of a shirt button, or the discovery of a stain upon their otherwise immaculate linen, it would have a wholesome tendency, and serve to correct some of her extravagant notions.[49]

Emily thought that if writing was to convey religious truth and not just be for amusement, men and women must be represented as

---

[46] June 19, 1866.

[47] June 19, 1866.

[48] Susan Warner and her sister Anna were evangelicals who wrote religious fiction, children's fiction, and theological works. Anna wrote the words for the hymn "Jesus Loves Me" for Susan's novel *Say and Seal*.

[49] April 20, 1866.

they are, not as they are fancied to be. All of Miss Warner's best characters were men who seemed to "elevate the opposite sex." Emily wrote, "Whether my woman nature feels piqued by this slight, or whether it is really unjust, I do not like it, for I do not believe it to be true that women are inferior to men in purity and strength. But I shall not quarrel with Miss W. after spending so many pleasant hours in her company."[50]

Reading the *Life of Hannah Moore* deepened Emily's appreciation for the Christian character of the English writer, educator, and philanthropist. She had thought Miss Moore of a cold, repressive nature, but found she was a lady of remarkable talents whose conversation and wit charmed Dr. Samuel Johnson and famed Shakespearean actor David Garrick. She was also admired by leaders such as Edmund Burke, John Newton, and William Wilberforce, whose philanthropic activities she shared. Emily noted,

> It is a striking commentary to the worth of religion when a nature, such as hers was, settles down in the meridian of life to a calm deliberate choice of God and his work. She had tried the blandishments of society, she had quaffed the cup of pleasure, delicate and high handed compliments had been offered her. She had known the satisfaction of pleasing, as well as being pleased; but she turned from every allurement to a simple life of faith. The intensity of her religious fervor is the peculiar charm which overshadows her latest years. She was born in 1745 and died in 1828.[51]

Horatius Bonar's *Words to the Winners of Souls* brought Emily to such an "exalted and delightful frame of mind" that it was difficult returning to the "low level of merely temporal enjoyment. Having once trod the mountain tops, why do we so cling to the

---

[50] April 20, 1866.
[51] April 25, 1866.

valleys? Having once caught a glimpse of our Saviour's countenance, how can we look elsewhere?" By Bonar setting forth so much of Emily's own experiences, his admonishments under difficulties were more easily accepted. Whatever the gloom and dark of night, she knew that another had encountered it before her, and she was not alone. In part through the writings of Bonar, eighteenth century Puritans and nonconformists such as Richard Baxter, Jonathan Edwards, Robert Murray McCheyne, and Phillip Doddridge all became friends who had shown the path before. Emily especially felt a kinship with Doddridge:

> I cannot tell the outline of his features, I know not whether his forehead was broad or high, whether his countenance was beautiful or repulsive, whether his manner was grace or cheerful, abrupt or polished, but of his spirit I know more, and knowing the spirit I know all that is worth knowing of any man. I know that he was often under the chisel, that he did not become a "polished stone" until blow after blow threatened to shatter the whole mass in fragments, It was through "great tribulation" that he came up to take his place among the hundred forty-four thousand.[52]

Emily's reading seemed to alternate between works of theological devotion and fiction. After she finished reading Victor Hugo's *Les Miserables* (which had first appeared during the Civil War), Emily asked herself, "how much of it can I carry away with me to weld into my character and become part of my future life? How can I sift it so as to retain the fine flour and throw away the bran?" She found the plot ingenuous and the book abounding in fertility of thought: "The author never speaks merely for the sake of saying something, it is always because he has something to say." The diction was beautiful, with just the right words to

---

[52] May 13, 1866.

express the meaning. The characters were well sustained. Yet, Emily found *Les Mesirables* a godless book:

> There is indeed a God represented but it is the God of infidel France and not the God of revelation. The man who wrote *Les Miserables* had not a just concept of God in his soul or he would never have attributed falsehood to Sister Simplice and then suppose that she would find them set down to her credit in paradise. I have little hesitation in saying that he believes in that universal salvation of his race. It is indicated again and again through the book. Hence I say the religious character of the book is bad. Some unthinking minds might read the book without making this discovery, but no lover of Jesus could do it.[53]

In concluding her critique, Emily wrote, "I do not think the book has injured me, it has been a kind of intellectual stimulant and I have enjoyed it, but I shall consider well the character of the person to whom I recommend it."

In August 1866, Emily, Milton and the boys took their summer vacation and went to Middlebury to visit with friends and relatives and attend the graduation at Middlebury College, as well as the inauguration of the new college president. Emily's journal is filled with vivid descriptions of the journey and the passengers encountered along the way – the long wait in the railway station, the middle aged lady looking for acquaintances in Canaan, the two ladies so lovely to look at, the woman who "had one of those uneasy tongues that are never quite satisfied with themselves except when in motion." After describing these so that the reader of Emily's journal can almost picture them today, Emily wrote,

> I have not the smallest idea that I made a sufficient impression upon any one of my fellow passengers that day

---

[53] June 29, 1866.

either in car or stagecoach to insure a single afterthought concerning me, and yet I have brought home those strangers to my chambers and to my musings and made them my companions for many days.[54]

The Severances took the train from Boscawen to Bethel and a stage coach from there to Hancock. They rose early in the morning to be driven over the mountains by an old man with a wooden leg. Emily rejoiced in the natural beauty surrounding them:

Those who have never climbed the Green Mountains know little of their wonder-working influence. Up, up, up in the summer glory and bewilderment. Gradually the mists rolled away and the sunlight crept into the silver brooks and among the quivering leaves making an entanglement of light and shade which in a picture we should call artistic but here in the grand old woods and in the great loving bosom of Nature is simply rapturous. I know not what can be of more interest to an artist than these depths of forest. The matted   undergrowth. The old logs decaying under their velvet mosses, the singing brooks, and chirping squirrels and noisy birds and fronded ferns. Every swelling of the breeze is a   new picture with its shifting light and varying colors. If I were a painter I am sure I should take my easel into the woods, and dip my brush in the rainbow and mix my colors with the brooks and never be satisfied until I could hang the live trees upon my canvass, and make the leaves rustle and the birds sing.[55]

She was certain this ride would be the most delightful aspect of her vacation. This was as close as possible to human happiness, for Emily knew perfect happiness was impossible now:

---

[54] August 1, 1866.
[55] August 1, 1866.

We say to ourselves we <u>should</u> be happy if it were not for something else which lies like a dull weight upon our hearts, which we cannot remove, and beyond which we may not pass. But this something else is to us an impassable gulf, we cannot bridge it over, we may not if we could. It chafes and cankers and corrodes, while it whispers evermore "this is not your rest."[56]

At Middlebury and Salisbury there were times of visiting with kinsmen and friends. Emily mentioned the rounds of visiting, blackberrying, picking peas, washing clothes, the ordination of Rev. Clark Mead in Cornwall, and the swirl of events surrounding the inauguration of Dr. Harvey Kitchell as the new President of Middlebury College. She especially enjoyed the address by Professor Edwards Amasa Parks of Andover on the importance of ministers of the gospel in remedying the moral wastes of the country. In the evening, Emily attended the President's Levee which the *New York Times* described as "A very pleasant social gathering in the spacious mansion and grounds of Mrs. Wainwright, which were opened for this purpose. A large company were assembled, and those who were familiar with the company, it was accounted one of the most pleasant incidents of the Commencement."[57] Yet, for Emily, it was a "miserable night," and she wrote, "the night of the happy crowd made me feel alone and unhappy more than I can express."[58] The cause of this aloneness in the midst of the happy throng Emily never reveals, but throughout her diary there is this strain of loneliness and pain that surfaces repeatedly. We can speculate about the cause, but without Emily clearly revealing it to us, we can never truly know its source.

---

[56] August 1, 1866. Hebrews 4:11.
[57] "Commencement, Middlebury College," *The New York Times*, August 13, 1866.
[58] August 8, 1866.

About a month after the visit to Middlebury, Emily wrote of her time alone with her Lord which brought relief to her melancholy and renewed her commitment to the work set before her:

> Sep 13th. There is so much exhilaration in the air this morning that I think I am on the whole more elevated than depressed, though there is an aching in my heart sadly at variance with the buoyant winds and the bright sunshine. ... They who have never staggered under a great sorrow cannot know the educational influences which lie wrapped up within it. How it prostrates the soul in the very depths of humiliation, and strips it of the selfish habiliments with which it is wont to be clothed until agonized and despairing it utters the cry, "Not my will but thine be done." ... That face, transfigured by a sorrow that has racked my being from center to circumference, I have seen. I am not using the language of ecstasy or of enthusiasm, but I have been alone with that Face in the cloud, so alone that no human sympathy could reach me, so abject nothing but Omnipotence could save me. ... . I have loved my Savior before but I have never been wholly alone with Him before. Two revelations have been made to me, a human soul laid bare and horrible in the sight of God and a Savior matchless enough in his perfections to lift that soul out of its corruption and clothe it in the garments of purity. I believe I have never so fully realized as now the compass of my life-work. I think my purpose was never so fully formed to thrust in the sickle and work with my might while the day lasts.[59]

In her period of melancholy darkness, Jesus was her "most intimate and best beloved Friend."

---

[59] September 13, 1866. Matthew 26:39

The Story of Emily

At the end of the year, Emily looked back over the months and again referred to this undefined darkness in her life, yet also the intimacy with Christ she experienced through the darkness:

> I feel as if I was sailing around Cape Horn and in hope some time to get back to the tropics. It has been in some respects the most eventful as well as the saddest year of my life – not outwardly, the sun has shown and the flowers have blossomed for me as usual, but within there has been a sky in which there was neither east nor west, morning nor midday, and whose only light came from the Star of Bethlehem. If I could write out upon these pages the experiences that have burned into my soul and desolated it of worldly joys, I should be better able to tell what Christ has done for me, but such experiences belong to the books that are not opened in this life, and I can only say that in the thick darkness He has been near me, my most intimate and best beloved Friend.[60]

Emily's journal reveals her inward life and thoughts and occasionally mentions those endless duties which consumed so much of her time. There were weddings (Marianne Webster's and Mathis Pillsbury's) and funerals (Mrs. Knowles') to attend, visitors to the town and parsonage, and visiting preachers to house. Then there was the ironing, meal preparations, and sewing clothes for the family. As she looked back upon one summer when she wrote nothing in her journal for three months, she noted that there had been endless work and activity accompanied by much quiet joy. Much of the time had been spent in needlework:

> none of your fancy fandangos but real serviceable articles, sheets, table cloths, napkins, shirts, pants, vests, coats, tucked dresses, plain dresses, and embroidered dresses for the baby, good dresses, calico dresses, muslin dresses, and silk dresses

---

[60] December 31, 1866.

for self, comfortables, dressing gowns, and innumerable articles which have escaped my memory at this moment. My blandest [gentlest] courtesy is due to Wheeler & Wilson, [sewing machine company] without whose aid I could never have accomplished so much in so short a time.[61]

There was also the help to train and supervise. Emily continued the New England practice from early Puritan days of having a girl to help in the kitchen and with domestic chores. The girl lived with the family, worked under Emily's training and supervision, and received some tutoring by Emily as well. Several girls came and went in the Severance household. One November Emily wrote in exasperation:

If ever I should write a book the subject of which should be "Hired Help," the present occupant of my kitchen would certainly come in for her rightful share of attention. It is therefore without malice of intent that I make mention here of her delicate hands never made for clothes wringers, her greasy dishwater and amazingly slow movements. "O passi graviora; dabit Deus his quoque finem."[62]

Emily did not feel at all adequate with the "mission work which needed to be done" with another girl, and she was thankful when the girl grew homesick and decided to leave her employ. Another girl was a petted child from Boston, who acknowledged she "did not know how to wash or cook or clean, paint or sew or do scarcely anything that needs to be done in a family like ours." Yet, she had a very amiable disposition and was willing to learn. She was, however, very heedless, "using buckwheat instead of flour for gingerbread, throwing soap grease into my jar of sweet pickles, breaking lamp chimneys by the dozen, burning up all the

[61] August 14, 1868.
[62] From Aeneas's words to his men in the *Aeneid* I.199: "Men who have endured weightier things, the god will give an end to these things also."

tin dishes in the house, and baking the sponge for bread on the overheated soap stove."[63] Yet, she did learn to make good biscuits, was very kind to the children, and "one of the most affectionate creatures alive." In short, "The good qualities on the whole overbalance her defects."

In September, Emily and Milton traveled the twenty-two miles to Bristol to visit Rev. Charles Abbott, a classmate of Milton's from Middlebury who also went to Andover. Rev. Abbott had pastored the church in Bristol for five years, but had to resign because of tuberculosis afflicting his lungs.[64] When Emily and Milton arrived at the Abbott home, they were met by Mrs. Abbott with the news that her husband had died the previous week and was buried. Emily and Milton spent a quiet hour with Harriet, the bereft widow, learning of Rev. Abbott's last weeks, days, and hours. Though he did not want to leave his work or his wife of three years, he told her, "If Jesus is willing that I should lay my armor by can you wonder Hattie that my heart bounds at the thought?" When he knew he was at the point of death, he went to his knees beside his bed, had his wife pray with him with his head upon her arms, and breathed his last. Mrs. Abbott showed Milton and Emily her husband's study, the garden he laid out, and the flowers he loved. As they left, Emily kissed Harriet warmly, bade her goodbye, and assured her she would always treasure the times with her:

> We turned away as from a shrine where holy memories lingered. We were mournful but there was triumph in our mourning. We felt that something sweet and sacred had gone from earth but not from us, for it was added to our thought of the life which is immortal. We had not lost more than we had gained, for if human life seemed less desirable, heaven seemed

---

[63] January 29, 1867.
[64] Richard Musgrave. *History of the Town of Bristol, Grafton Co., N.H.* Bristol, N.H.: R.W. Musgrave, 1904, 1.

more dear. The aggregate of our happiness was not lessened, while that of his was infinitely increased. His meek resigning of the armor, his triumphant passage over Jordan are food in the strength of which our souls ought to go rejoicing many days.[65]

Emily rejoiced in the natural beauty of Vermont, a beauty frequently described in her journal as leading to reflections on spiritual truths. One October evening she wrote,

The wild atmosphere and the gorgeous woods this afternoon put me into sympathy with Nature which is exquisite. I am ready to stop my breath and listen for the soft throbbing of her bosom. I touch the yellow leaves with something like an expectation that I shall come upon a beating pulse. My ear is open to her unclosed harmonies. My spirit drinks in this Autumn sweetness, until it is fairly intoxicated with delight. Is there not something in this appeal of the inanimate to the animate which hints at and dimly prefigures immortality? Do not these virgin harmonies create a longing for and suggest the possibility of harmonies that shall be unending? Does not the fellowship of feeling between the different creations argue strongly that they are the work of our Creator? and if of one, of an infinite One? And cannot an Infinite One carry forward and perfect his finite creations in infinity? And if one of these creations is then carried forward and made perfect how can we limit God's goodness by saying that others shall not be? What assurance have we that this "new heavens and new earth" of which we read in scripture may not be these heavens and this earth purified and refitted for the reception of the immortal life of the soul? We do read that the earth shall be burned up, but fire is the favorite element employed in scripture as an instrument of purification, and moreover science has

---

[65] September 26, 1866.

demonstrated that particles of matter are not destroyed but only change in form by the action of fire upon them. Now can we tell that these same particles may take to themselves new and spiritual forms, even as the particles of the body which are now clothed with corruption shall rise from the grave and put on incorruptible. It is a beautiful thought to me that I may yet meet these same trees bearing no longer the stain of the fall upon them, that I may possibly drink in the beauty of these flowers which I cannot conceive more perfect but which may be spiritualized and made harmonious with a higher order of existence. That I may yet roam over these hills and recognize them as the places where I met the toil and joy and discipline of mortal life. Viewed in this light the associations of place to which we cling with such tenacious fondness are no idle waste of sentiment. Each one shall bring to us a purer joy than we have known when we see it in the light of all God's providences, and mark how out of numberless possibilities we chose the identical ones which should bring us into unison with God's plans.[66]

Emily also found intense joy and peace in the weekly Sabbath. The New England, Puritan Sabbath was different from all other days, and Emily "looked with different eyes on that day." Nature itself became transfigured:

Whether storms lash the forests, or mists hurry up the hills or the sunshine lies full and clear upon the meadows, it is all the same – a thought of God. And when I turn my eyes inward upon my own heart – then too I see more clearly its deformity, I am better able to strip the false robes from my sins and expose the skeletons, better able to see the necessity of being

---

[66] October 8, 1866. Revelation 21-22; II Peter3:10; I Corinthians 15:50-55.

"clothed upon," and how salvation must be <u>all of grace</u>. Thank God for the Sabbath! [67]

When the children were infants, Emily usually stayed home with them during the morning service, allowing the servant girl to attend the service. In the afternoon, the servant kept the children, and Emily attended worship. Sabbath evening was a family time of teaching the children their Scripture verses and Bible stories, reading the Scriptures and devotional books, and singing hymns together. Emily recorded her reflections on one Sabbath day:

I sat down by the east window and looked out upon the cold sky, the river, and the bleak hills. My thoughts naturally grouped themselves around my recent reading and study, in which I have conceived of the human mind in the exercise of the loftiest activities, enlarged and disciplined by study and illuminated by grace, as some feeble foreshadowing of the Divine mind, and it has seemed to me that the nearer we can come to the knowledge, and beauty, and dignity, and grace, and activity of these noble minds, the more just and adequate must be our conception of the Divine mind, not but that we have in the passion of Jesus a complete humanity, but it is so complete that we need stepping stones to lead us up to it, how much <u>more</u> when we attempt to conceive of his Divinity. For my own part I have thought so much of the weak, pitiful suffering character of the Savior that I am in danger of forgetting that in him was the most consummate intellect, the most delicate fancy, the grandest will. But when I think of Newton and Shakespeare and Kant – and Dr. Judson and remember that all I admire and love them for, exists in infinite perfection in the Divine mind, it assists my struggling conceptions and brings me nearer to it.[68]

---

[67] October 28, 1866. II Corinthians 5:1-5; Ephesians 2:8.
[68] October 28, 1866.

The Story of Emily

A poem Emily wrote about the Sabbath appeared in *The Vermont Historical Gazetteer* in 1867:

The First Sabbath

Morn broke in beauty o'er a world,
    Fresh from the touch of Heaven,
And ushered in the day of rest,
    Which crowned the perfect seven.
And from the new-born world arose
    Upon the morning air,
This grateful, oft-repeated strain
    Of true and fervent prayer,
                "Praise God."

The morning stars that gemmed the arch
    Of heaven's unfathomed blue,
Together sang their hymns of joy,
    And trimmed their fires anew,
While all their harps the sons of God
    Tuned to a new employ,
And o'er that first, sweet Sabbath calm,
    Shouted the song of joy,
                "Praise God."

In all their awful majesty
    The lofty mountains stood,
Their jutting rocks, all covered o'er
    With moss and tangled wood;
And from each cliff and craggy peak,
    One peel of gladness came,
Till all the valleys caught the sound,
    And echoed back the same.
                "Praise God."

The flowers a tinge of vermeil caught,
    While tremblingly they stood,
As if they blushed to hear their God
    Pronounce them "very good;"
And from their dew-bathed petals rose
    An incense pure on high,
And from their gently parted lips
    The sweet, but mute reply,
                        "Praise God."

Man, too majestic in his strength,
    And woman, sweet as fair,
Went forth and laid their sacrifice
    Upon the altar there.
The noblest ones that walked the earth,
    All sinless, and all blest,
Sent up the homage of their hearts
    On that first day of rest.
                        "Praise God." [69]

Emily knew that the shaping of her children's character was an important responsibility, and she carefully studied her children's distinct natures. Claude had "a tender affectionate heart, a good deal of moral power for one so young, buoyant spirits, and an enthusiastic manner." Willie was very different. Full of life and fun, he made "a most original use of the King's English."[70] Milton one day reproved Emily for not teaching Willie more, and Emily recommended that Milton set the example. So, the father began to

---

[69] Mrs. E.A. Severance. "The First Sabbath," *The Vermont Historical Gazatteer*, ed. Abby Maria Hemenway. Vol. I. Burlington, Vermont, 1867, 93. Emily's poem was one of the essays and poems contributed from West Salisbury.
[70] February 9, 1867.

teach the little one the New England children's prayer, "Now I lay me down to sleep." When Milton told Willie to repeat each line, Willie inserted his father's name throughout, beginning with the first line, "Now papa lay papa down to sleep." Milton never reproved Emily again about Willie's instruction. However, Emily could not help but be concerned about the child's future, since he was so slow to learn.

Emily had once thought that children were what their teachers had made them. However, once she had children of her own to train, she found that their individual natures contributed as well. Willie was a difficult child to manage; Claude had a more determined will. Then, August 14, 1867, a new little lamb, Carlton Spencer, was added to the fold. It required a great deal of strength and care to give her three boys all the spiritual training needed. Yet, Emily wrote that

> God will not put more work in my hands than He will give me strength to do, or patience to see undone, and therefore I will not despond, but I long for a greater tact in understanding and influencing these children. It seems to me that it must be partly my fault that they are no more like what I would have them, and yet I have tried my utmost to teach them propriety. … "Who is sufficient for these things?" May the pain I feel at witnessing the imperfections of my children remind me that I have a <u>Father</u> who is wounded at every deviation of mine from the path of duty.[71]

"Claudie's Prayer," a poem Emily wrote about one of her mothering experiences, later appeared in the "Letter Box" of the children's magazine *Our Young Folks*:

Claudie's Prayer
"Come, Claudie, the bird in the maple

---

[71] September 28, 1867. II Corinthians 9:8; 2:16; 12:9

Has ended her motherly cares,
And kitty is purring in dreamland,
'Tis time you were saying your prayers."

But Claudie's feet never grew weary,
His eyes were too starlike for sleep,
And off in the garden he bounded
With many a frolicsome leap.

Life bubbled within and ran over
In ripples of laughter and fun,
Unconscious of self or its action,
As the hat or the dress he had on.

"Come, Claudie," I said, as I found him
Coiled up in a strange little heap,
"Your fresh milk and night-gown are waiting, -
'Tis time you were taking your sleep."

But Caudie still wriggled, and twisted,
And floundered in infinite glee,
Till vexed at myself for forbearance
I grew near as childish as he.

"Come, Claudie," I said, and impatience
Looked everywhere out of my eyes,
As I added somewhat to my wrinkles
And tried to look dreadfully wise.

His rosy lip quivered a moment,
His little round hand was in mine,
And into the parlor in silence
I led him with settled design.

Then barring his eyes to the twilight,
He fell on his bare little knees,
And I thought that some bright shining angel
Dropped the words in his mouth, - they were
        these: -

"God bless my mamma," – and the accents
Were mingled with sobbing and tears,
And the prayer went no further in utterance,
Though I think that it reached to His ears.

He said not a word of "Our Father,"
Not a word of his "Now I lay me,"
And I thought in the hush of that moment
That I needed the prayer more than he.

And oft in the days that have followed,
When life has grown somber with care,
Impatience and weakness have vanished
At the thought of that night and that prayer.[72]

Emily received $3.00 for her poem.

In the midst of caring for the children, her household
responsibilities, and responsibilities in the Boscawen church,
whenever she had opportunity, Emily read. Often her reading time
was on the Sabbath and consisted of spiritual and devotional
works. She recorded her thoughts about books she read in her
journal, since, as she wrote,

> unfortunately for my purpose the faculty called memory has
> shown some reluctance to transporting all the ponderous packs

---

[72] Mrs. E. A. Severance, "Claudie's Prayer," *Our Young Folks*, Vol. III. Boston,
June, 1867, 384.

which I am inclined to put upon her shoulders. I see no way of mending the matter except by trying to assist her in her drudgery, and I trust she will give me due credit for the few items which I shall register here.[73]

Within months after its publication she read the anonymous *Ecce Homo*, a treatment of the humanity of Christ. Emily noted that the work had "come as near to turning the religious world upside down as any mere human production often does." At the time, there was much conjecture as to who the author was. Most agreed he was not a minister. Emily judged him to be an Episcopalian:

> He speaks as if men were converted by a process of education as if the work of the Holy Spirit was to infuse an enthusiasm into Christ's followers. The work is in no sense a life of Christ, but it treats of him as the founder of a society, explains or endeavors to what his object was and how far it was attained. He evidently has an intellectual belief in Christ, but his heart does not seem to have been drawn out in love and worship for him.[74]

Milton considered the work an attack on Christianity in that the author valued the ethical teachings and example of Christ without acknowledging his deity and redemptive work. Emily didn't think the author an infidel, but certainly full of inconsistencies. The author later revealed himself as Sir John Robert Seeley, professor of Latin at University College, London and his *Ecce Homo* is recognized as an early proponent of liberal theology.

Emily especially enjoyed biographies and memoirs, writing, "They seem to me like introductions to persons whom I expect to know hereafter, and the more I can learn of them now the more

---

[73] October 8, 1866.
[74] October 8, 1866.

will my interest in them be enhanced when I come to know them personally."[75] The restful Sabbath was when Emily most often read Christian biographies. These included the *Memoirs of Thomas Chalmers*, the Scottish divine of the early 19th century and leader of the Evangelical party. His passion for the Scriptures and bringing souls to the Lord was coupled with his educational work in promoting religion and moral improvement.[76] Several times over the years Emily read Fidelia Fiske's *Recollections of Mary Lyon*, the founder of Mount Holyoke. Each reading deepened Emily's impression of Mary Lyon's character and her own desire to be more like her:

> The sound, sweet, healthy values of a matron like hers is very rare, and after perusing the history of the Churches from the landing of the Pilgrims until the present time one is tempted to exclaim, "Of the daughters of New England many have done virtuously, but thou excellest them all."[77]

The *Memoirs of William Ellery Channing* both pleased and pained Emily.[78] She admired his "nobility of soul" and "remarkable mental power," as well as his "high sense of honor" and "freedom from self adulation." His "misconception of the character of Christ" pained her. Though Channing was a champion among the Unitarians, Emily did not believe he would have sympathy with the Unitarians of her day, which were strongly influenced by Transcendentalism and German rationalism.

Emily read works of literature on non-Sabbath days, but even then she analyzed the work for its literary and spiritual value. She thought Edward Ward Beecher's *Norwood* delineated the New

---

[75] May 23, 1868.
[76] October 28, 1866.
[77] November 17, 1867. Proverbs 31:29.
[78] May 23, 1868.

England character as effectively as Hugo's *Les Miserables* had the French character.[79]

The new year of 1867, brought a renewal in the Boscawen church. Attendance grew. Some seriously inquired, "What must I do to be saved?" The faces of others "glowed with the love of God which for a long time glowed with self and the world." As Milton faithfully preached and ministered among the people, Emily wished she could do more to help him in his work. She did pray for him and the efficacy of his ministry and was astonished "sometime to see how much my husband depends upon my prayers."[80]

Emily could look back on the deep melancholy which had enshrouded her the previous year and be thankful for the peace which again pervaded her soul. She hoped that she would be more like-minded with Christ, and that her children would know more of Christ by seeing her life. As Claudie began attending the district school, Emily dreaded the morals to which he was exposed, though she thought they could still guard him in these young teachable years. She was concerned that little Willie was slow to learn, yet he was full of precious sayings. One day he came in all animated, describing some birds he had seen in his neighbor's trees, "those trees that reached way up to where God lives."[81] Another day she overheard Willie asking Claudie how they would get all their playthings to God's house when they went to live with Him. Emily wrote that "the one wish of my heart for my children is that they may take Christ for their Friend before they bid adieu to their childhood, so that they may have a safeguard against the temptations of youth."[82]

---

[79] April 16, 1868.
[80] January 1867. Acts 16:30
[81] August 9, 1867.
[82] August 15, 1968

When Emily turned thirty, March 24, 1868, she rejoiced in the Lord's closeness, writing,

> I have done little to celebrate the day except to indulge in a little worsted work which possibly may live when I am gone. My conscience has been clear and in that I am beginning more and more to find my happiness. If I can only feel sure that the Lord is on my side, other things must not, and shall not make me permanently unhappy. I think I have never felt more fully than at the present time that <u>Christ</u> is my <u>All</u>. I am thoroughly tired of the world's heartlessness, and am more than ever determined to make my life <u>mean something</u>. When I lie under the green sod which shall cover me in a few more years may it be said that my life meant purity, simplicity, industry, and earnestness. Let my children remember me as instilling these virtues into their youthful minds and I can ask no loftier monument. I am not as buoyant as I used to be. I seem to myself to have outlived my hopes and anticipations. I take each day as it comes and try to improve and enjoy it and the rest I leave with God. Henceforth my pleasure shall be in doing my duty.

Boscawen was in the vicinity of Daniel Webster's home of Marshfield, and when relatives came to visit in the summer, Emily and Milton took them to visit Daniel Webster's boyhood home, accompanied by some friends and members from church who were related to the famous statesman. Claudie climbed the old oak tree where the young Daniel hung his scythe. Emily was most impressed with the magnificent spreading elm overshadowing the house – the elm spread "a hundred feet from the farthest twig on the north to the farthest on the south and eighteen feet around the trunk."[83] John Taylor, who had worked for Daniel Webster for over twenty years and was with him days before his death, took the

---

[83] August 14, 1968.

group around the property and shared his personal remembrances of Webster with them. They all enjoyed a lovely picnic before taking the pleasant, quiet ride home in the early evening.

In October Emily and Milton attended the annual meeting of the American Board of Commissioners of Foreign Missions in Norwich, Connecticut. On the way they enjoyed some time in Boston visiting the Boston Museum and Athenaeum. Emily especially enjoyed the mummies, Chinese work, and model of the French Guillotine at the Museum; at the Athenaeum she especially found interesting the paintings of the embarking of the Pilgrims, a scene in the Coliseum in Rome, and the handwriting on the wall at Belshazzar's feast. Milton took a train to East Abington, where he was to preach, while Emily stayed in Boston. Sunday she attended the Episcopal service in the morning, the North Church in the afternoon, and the Methodist church in the evening. She thought the Methodist preacher "possessed more imagination than prudence."

The meeting of the A.B.C.F.M. was filled with notable presentations and times of prayer. One morning Emily attended the first anniversary of the Woman's Board of Missions, and several interesting ladies addressed the meetings. Emily wrote, "I think it eminently appropriate for ladies to conduct meetings like these among themselves but whenever they do so they demonstrate their unfitness to take charge of public gatherings generally."[84]

Though the Boscawen Church witnessed a number of conversions and an increase in membership, there was a disharmony in the church in these years following the Civil War. Some were bringing politics into the church and focusing on political issues rather than the cause of Christ. When Milton attended the bed of a dying member of his congregation, the man's last words to him were, "Now there will be one less Republican."

---

[84] November 15, 1868.

Politics seemed to consume everyone and was producing a disharmony among the people. Unable to overcome the discord, Milton tendered his resignation on December 13, 1868. He had been offered the pastorate of the church in Orwell, Vermont.

Leaving their home and friends in Boscawen brought tears to Emily's eyes. Every room in the house was filled with so many memories:

> The Study! – oh the stories which these silent walls might tell if once they should break into sound! Here have been heard the repentant sighs of those who have sought the way of the Cross, and here have ascended earnest prayers in their behalf. Here have been sacred confidences and many pleasant social reunions. Above all here has the "well-beaten oil" been prepared for the sanctuary, and often from these windows the light has flickered far into the night, while a solitary occupant has girded himself anew for his life work.

Memories flooded over her as she looked one last time into the various rooms. Many who had gathered around their dining room table would not be seen again:

> We must form new acquaintances and interest ourselves in a new strange people….May God in mercy be with us when we find ourselves alone with aching hearts among strangers. The new field seems promising but I feel afraid of it, or rather I feel afraid of myself.[85]

Looking at her new home in Orwell seemed to Emily "like a mountain to be scaled."

---

[85] December 27, 1868.

Chapter 3 – A Growing Family in Orwell

"And let us not be weary in well doing;
for in due season we shall reap if we faint not." ~ Galatians 6:9

Emily was not unacquainted with the village of Orwell. Her mother had been born and raised there, and there were many cousins still in the community. Even so, moving into a new home was a challenge. When they first arrived at the parsonage on January 5, 1869, it was pouring down rain. The people were warm and friendly, but the furniture and carpets didn't fit. New furniture had to be ordered. Emily became ill the next day, but

> Jesus was such a blessed Comforter that I found it sweet to be in his arms. And it was so sweet to meet him there, so soon, in our new dwelling that I tried not to care for any discouragements which might come. I said to myself if <u>He</u> will only dwell with us here I can be happy all the day long. And I <u>was</u> happy.[86]

Her new house did not suit Emily perfectly, but she didn't expect one to do so until she came to "My father's house on high." There would be no dripping stove pipes there! – "not only will love

---

[86] January 17, 1869.

and hope and faith find the fulfillment of their longings but taste also will be gratified and no more be subject to the offense of unwelcome sight and sounds."

The Orwell Congregational Church meetinghouse was in a Greek revival style and was among the most beautiful in Vermont. After the Civil War, the congregation took up a subscription and installed a Hook tracker organ to honor returning Civil War veterans. Milton was installed as pastor of this Congregational Church on February 3, 1869. Dr. Kitchel, President of Middlebury College, and Rev. Winchester, husband of Milton's sister Mary Catherine, were among the clergy officiating. Emily enjoyed the ceremony and sermons and felt at home with the people, who were very warm to them.

During the move, Emily continued to seek to nurture the boys in the Scriptures. She was especially concerned about Willie, who seemed dull and unable to comprehend what was taught him, even simple Bible verses. One evening, she became so disheartened that she lay down on the lounge and let the tears come. She told Jesus of her weakness, impatience, and inefficiency in teaching the little ones and asked Him to help her find a way into their hearts. At that moment, Carrie, the girl who was helping Emily with the housework, began sweetly singing across the room, "My faith looks up to Thee, Thou Lamb of Calvary, Savior Divine." The words took away Emily's burdens to the foot of the Cross. It seemed to confirm the Scripture, "Before they call upon me I will answer and while they are yet speaking I will hear." (Isaiah 65:24): "How delightful to verify those promises in our own experience, to prove for ourselves independent of Nature and Reason, that the Word of God is true, not merely to believe it, but to know it."[87]

When the children came in and saw Emily's tears, she explained their cause, which seemed to have a quieting influence

---

[87] February 14, 1869.

on them. Claudie said he would try to please the Savior and be His own little child. Later in the afternoon, when she was reading to him of a little boy who gave his burden of sin to Jesus, Claudie said, "O, I should not think that would be the right way. I should give the burden of sin to Satan, and give the <u>love</u> to Jesus."

Emily desired to be useful for Christ in her new home, especially praying for a Sabbath School Class and a ladies' prayer meeting. By the end of April her prayer was providentially answered when Mrs. Catlin, who had taught a class of young ladies, was called away to help her aged parents in Shoreham and asked Emily to take over teaching the class. Emily would be teaching about twenty young ladies, varying in age from 18 to 22. She felt the class was a special gift from God to her: "I fully expect that the new position will be one which I shall greatly enjoy. Jesus gives it to me and I can but feel that He will add His blessing, if I am only faithful."[88]

In a letter to Mount Holyoke alumnae, Emily reflected on the ten years which had passed since the Class of '58 had said their farewells. Emily had kept in touch with many of her classmates, and she reflected on those in the class who had already gone upward:

> While we compare our varied fortunes, and wonder at the strange providences through which we have been led, they sit together in heavenly places and spend the joyful years in unmingled delight. In all breadth and energy of thought, we are more dead than they. In all holy activities of soul, they are more alive than we… they inhabit the mansions in our Father's house….
>
> As we ply our journey hither and thither, across the mountains and prairies of the continent, in search of our scattered sisters,

---

[88] April 25, 1869.

we find most of them in their chosen nook, ready to respond to our eager questioning: but as we turn our eyes upward, no answer comes from the silent heavens to our pleading…We listen, and the only sounds we catch are the words, 'Thou knowest not now, but thou shalt know hereafter." We can well afford to wait.[89]

Emily thoroughly enjoyed her Sabbath Class of young ladies, though sometimes she wondered if she could truly elevate them intellectually and spiritually. During one lesson, she noticed one of the married ladies in the class actually looking for first Corinthians in the Old Testament. Emily wrote, "Surely heathenism is at our doors, and we must meet it here. The question is how?"[90] One lesson Emily found particularly delightful, and she copied some of the questions in her diary:

The Marriage of the King's Son
When is it going to be? Matt. 25:31, 32
Are there many invited? Is. 55:1
Are all our class going? Matt. 7:21
Will there be very many there? Rev. 7:9-10
Is it any honor to be invited? Rev. 19:7-9
How will the bride be dressed? Rev. 19:8
Can we get near enough to see her? Rev. 21:9-10
Will there be any music? Rev. 14:1-3
What shall we be expected to wear? I Peter 3:3-4
What if we shouldn't be dressed nice enough? Matt. 22:11-13
Will it be stylish to be a little late? Matt. 25:11-13
How will the King's Son be dressed? Rev. 1:13-16
Am I expected to bring anyone with me? Isa. 43:6; Dan. 12:3

---

[89] A clipping of this Mount Holyoke 1869 alumnae letter was pasted in the back of Emily's diary. John 14:2-4; John 13:7.
[90] May 23, 1869.

Will it be a costly feast? John 3:16; Isaiah 53:5;
Rev. 21:6, last clause
Should I be expected to help bear the expenses? Isa. 52:3
Will there be any mourners there? Rev. 21:4
Is there more than one entrance into the feast? John 10:1
Shall I be noticed there? Rev. 6:15-16
Will the feast be well lighted? Rev. 21:23-24; 22:5
What if we are not quite prepared? Rev. 22:11-12
How is the invitation worded? Rev. 22:17
Are there any rewards for those who accept? Rev. 22:14[91]

Though even Milton was not particularly supportive, Emily moved ahead in organizing a Ladies' Prayer meeting. After much "halting, and trembling, and fearing that it might not be a success," the first meeting was held the first of September:

Nobody gave me any encouragement, even my husband put me off for weeks thinking it needed the extra impulse of a sermon to stir the ladies up to the enterprise, but at last with a kind of desperation I determined we would make the trial and leave the result with God.[92]

Ten ladies came to the first meeting, only three of whom had ever been to a prayer meeting. The prayers were often hesitant and did not go beyond a few words, but this feeble beginning was full of promise. Emily was convinced more than ever that such a meeting was needed: "These women do not lack feeling, they do not lack thought, but they lack experience in giving expression to their thoughts, and they lack the assistance which comes from a mutual interchange of religious views." Emily was determined to continue with the meetings. Gradually, more women came, and their prayers became more fluent and expressive.

---

[91] November 28, 1869.
[92] September 19, 1869.

Emily relished the Sabbath rest, coming between the cares of the weeks:

> The great question is how to keep this world out, and how to let Christ into the heart. On other days I try to make room for both, the world comes rushing and jostling its way along and will have its share of attention, while Christ stands at the door, not pushing and elbowing his way into the heart by main force, but knocking, and imploring and waiting to be invited in, waiting for the doorkeeper to push aside the jostling crowd and make room for him. I don't think the Savior requires us to push the world entirely aside and shut ourselves in a hermit's cell with him, but I do think that we should have him so much in mind and heart that all the needful activities which belong to us as intellectual and social beings should become Christian in their character and influence. It is not so much the thing done, as the spirit in which it is done, which determines whether or not an act is Christian.[93]

As an example, Emily recounted that the previous week "one of the Lord's servants" came for dinner. As she prepared the table for dinner, Emily noticed the tablecloth was partly soiled, and she considered whether the dishes and mats might cover up the soiled spots. Then she thought,

> If the Savior were here in Orwell and was going to be my guest at dinner, how I would delight to spread for Him the finest of the linens. What a table I would set for Him! But quicker than I can write it came the answering thought, "Inasmuch as ye have done it unto me." Attentions paid to Mr. Smith were attentions paid to Him, I gathered up the soiled linen and putting it away for washing day, I commenced setting the table anew, as if I were doing it for my Savior. There was real enjoyment then in carrying on the simple preparations and when the meal was

---

[93] November 28, 1869. Revelation 3:20.

over and I removed the cloth from the table <u>it had not been soiled at all.</u> So I think we shall set our tables better, and sweep better and iron better and do all our work more faithfully if we carry Christ always about with us in our thoughts. "Always bearing about with us the dying of the Lord Jesus."[94]

In August, Emily and Milton routinely went to the commencement in Middlebury, attending the week of lectures and visiting old friends and relatives. Emily sometimes found these visits difficult. She was not one for small talk, and at the Levee at President Kitchell's, she often felt very much alone. The children enjoyed staying with the grandparents during this time, and it was rejuvenating to visit relatives and explore some of the beauties of the countryside. Emily especially enjoyed hiking up Snake Mountain, which was an easy climb:

It is shut up in by the woods, which tell us no new stories but charm us at every step with their oft repeated mysteries. There is the same overarching and interlacing of bough and branch which delighted my dreamy childhood, the same tremendous network with the sunshine dropping through the mysterious silences echoing with every human sound. The deep shadows and delicious sense of repose – They are all the same inscriptions which we find in the deep woods everywhere, sometimes carved more eloquently than at others but always legible to the real lover of Nature. We found no outlook on the way, and caught no glimpse of the lovely panorama which was to reward our toil until it burst upon us all at once from the open space at the summit. There range above range of the Adirondacks stretched away to edge the horizon, until in the dim distance we could not tell when the mountain ended and the sky began. Nestling at their feet and creeping up

---

[94] November 28, 1869. Matthew 25:45; II Corinthians 4:10.

their sides were the quiet villages which here and there enliven the Western shore of Lake Champlain.[95]

Willie said, "Snake Mountain was so high that it did not seem as it was more than a mile from the top of it up to God's house."

As Emily's life became busier and busier, often months separated her diary entries. There were endless rounds of engagements among the people, all the clothes to be sewn for the children and herself, as well as Milton's shirts. She spent one birthday making buttonholes on the twelve new shirts she had made for Milton. Then there was the cooking, washing, ironing, as well as the care of the children. There was little time for reading or study or writing. Though she often had a girl to help her in the kitchen, often times she did not. It was when overburdened with work that Milton proposed they take a trip west. He was chosen by his Church to attend the Pilgrim's Memorial Convention in Chicago, commemorating the two hundred and fiftieth anniversary of the landing of the Pilgrims at Plymouth in 1620. Milton thought after the convention they could then travel to Iowa, Minnesota, and other places out west, visiting relatives and friends. Both Milton and Emily corresponded regularly with many friends from their college days, as well as contacts they had made through the missionary and church meetings they attended.

Emily was nauseated by the frequent rocking of the boats and trains on the travel and often had ammonia to try to stave off the sickness, sometimes to no avail. Yet, Emily took an interest in the changing scenery and the numerous people met, describing them with verve and expressiveness in her diary a month after they returned home. There were one thousand people at the Pilgrim Convention, with Edward Beecher (son of Lyman and brother of Harriet Beecher Stowe) acting as moderator. Numerous addresses

---

[95] August 22, 1869.

rehearsed the history of the Pilgrims and Puritans and challenged the leaders present to follow their illustrious example of standing for truth.

After the Pilgrim Convention, Emily and Milton headed for Iowa, where Joseph Allen, Emily's older brother, and his wife Fidelia had established a farm in the 1850's. It was good to connect with them again, but getting to Iowa required more jarring and jolting on the steam cars. At last Emily could see "the wide, wide prairie of which I had heard so much and seen so little." Emily noted that Sunday "Milton preached of course, and of course I didn't." After a week with Joseph Allen, the couple took passage for St. Paul, Minnesota. Emily was captivated by the scenery:

> Up the Mississippi! How to take in this bold rugged scenery and impress it upon the mind so that it can never be obliterated is the problem which has been thrusting itself upon me for a day and a half. Can I make these green hills live in everlasting remembrance so that I can carry back to New England the Conic section of Sugar Loaf and the romantic beauty of Winona and Lover's Leap and introduce them as new acquaintances to my friends?[96]

At St. Paul, Emily and Milton visited with cousins and with alumni from Middlebury established in the city. There was an obvious atmosphere of growing success in the town, and Emily and Milton began looking for property they might invest in. At last they began the long journey home. Emily was feeling sick most of the way, and her ammonia bottle was always at hand.

The following summer was a busy one:

> …a continual attempt to keep even with the world, or more definitely to keep even with the demands for new garments,

---

[96] Emily wrote her account of the trip west on June 15, 1870.

and the impertinence of old ones, to keep patience with
unreasonable servants and to keep strength and courage with
none at all, to keep peaceful and apparently undisturbed when
there was no peace, to keep my heart warm and tender when
there was little to find warmth or tenderness and to keep my
faith in God unclouded when the heavens seemed brass and the
earth iron. Sometimes I have been almost ready to cry out,
"Hath God forgotten to be gracious, hath He in anger shut up
His tender mercies?", but within the last week I have had much
to convince me that He has not forgotten, that "having loved
His own He loves them to the end."[97]

Emily's Sabbath School Class made her a surprise visit and
brought her an elegant cake basket, something she had long desired
and which was doubly appreciated by its fond associations. Emily
had taught a Sabbath School Class at various times since she was
sixteen, but this class was the most enjoyable:

We have taken sweet counsel together and walked to the house
of God in company, and whenever I have tried to impress them
with the grand old truths of the revealed word I have been
conscious that those truths were rebounding with blessings
upon my own soul. Many a time I have taken my Bible with
the assigned lesson and gone forth feeling entirely inadequate
to add one word of explanation or analysis beyond the sacred
text, and at such times it has been my custom to breathe an
inward prayer that the Holy Spirit might illuminate for me the
sacred page and be my commentary and guide. And so asking I
have never come away empty; ideas would present themselves
to my mind with simplicity and clearness and words would not
be wanting to express them.[98]

---

[97] October 23, 1870. Psalm 77:9; John 13:1
[98] October 23, 1869.

November 28, 1870, "another sweet child" was added to the family when Maude Emily was born.[99] Emily trusted she would "add to our happiness through eternal ages." As she clasped the baby to her heart and pondered the child's future,

> I believe no other desire for her is so strong as that she may be kept "unspotted from the world." I would have her thoughts so pure that they might be inscribed upon her forehead in characters of light where all the world might see. In a world where there is so much sham, nothing is more beautiful, and I might add nothing is more rare – in woman than an <u>intelligent simplicity</u> and sincerity of character. That my little Maude may have this rare accomplishment is both my wish and prayer.[100]

As 1872 began, Emily described something of her life in Orwell in her letter to her Mount Holyoke classmates:

> We live in a quiet farming community but the people are intelligent, social, and appreciative, and the natural scenery through all this region is unsurpassed. Our family group is more perfect than it was, for a little daughter has been added to it. She is now thirteen months old. So if you would be introduced to my retinue, dear sisters, here they are: Claude, my oldest son, ten years of age, who has been through Greenleaf's Arithmetic, and is studying Latin; Wilbert, the second son, eight years of age, of whom it cannot yet be said "much learning hath made him mad," but if you want to build a jumper or sail a boat or have fun generally, he is just the boy for you. Number three is Carlton, four years old, with an unlimited capacity for wriggling himself out of a tight place;

---

[99] Emily's problems with motion sickness and nausea during the trip west were undoubtedly exacerbated by her being in the early weeks of her pregnancy with Maude. James 1:27.

[100] December 22, 1870. That Emily was in the early months of her pregnancy during her trip west would explain in part her constant suffering from nausea and motion sickness.

then Maude, the pet and darling of us all. My husband is in better health than formerly, and thoroughly enjoys his work among this people.[101]

Emily further encouraged her sisters spiritually to remember that "Truth is elevating, not depressing." The Christian indeed suffers times of humiliation and suffering, but we should lift high the standard of the cross "with joyful, exultant faith, and represent before the world" a robust piety.

With another little soul under her care, Emily continually prayed and wrestled with the upbringing of the children and her own inadequacies for the task. She often lacked patience with them, and thought if Jesus were as impatient with her, she would be continually "under the rod." Her desire was to fortify them against the evil in the world and that they might "grow up to be sturdy Christians, standing each one where Providence assigns a place to honor God and bless mankind."[102]

The boys were often a challenge. Claude was at a giggling stage and would not always apply himself to his studies. Carlton was almost unmanageable, though he was learning to read quickly at the age of five. Emily knew that if a child ever got the upper hand, parental authority could be lost forever. She didn't like to fight, but could not yield to an unreasoning child. It seemed every day she had to either stand her ground, or suffer defeat. Moral suasion seemed to have no effect upon them, and she knew a strong discipline was necessary. Emily hoped

…that I may not fail in the training of these children, for just now this is the work of my life. Everything else is subservient to this. If these children can only grow up to an honorable and useful maturity, I shall feel that I have not lived in vain. If they

[101] Letter to classmates from Orwell, Vt., January, 1872, from a clipping pasted in the back of Emily's diary.
[102] December 24, 1871.

do not, and only occupy a ciphers place in the community, ah me. What <u>shall</u> I do? May God be merciful and help me.[103]

Emily was determined that the boys would learn the lesson of obedience, but it took great effort. She prayed,

> Oh that the blessed influences of the Holy Spirit might be given as a guide to them and an assistant to me. Without it I know my best efforts will fail but with it I feel assured of final and glorious success. I feel almost overwhelmed sometimes with a sense of weakness and general unfitness for my work.[104]

Little Maude was of the sweetest disposition, but when she contracted whopping cough, she clung to Emily and wanted to be in her lap at all times. With the baby sick, Emily sent Milton and Claudie to the Middlebury commencement on their own, staying at home with Maude, Willie, and Carlton. Carlton had wanted to go to the Milk Factory for some time, so Emily let him go with Charlie Barrett. About an hour after he left, Deacon Wilcox drove up with little Carlton, bruised and pale, across his lap. Emily sent Willie for the doctor, cleaned up Carlton, and put him in bed. He was breathing very heavily. Apparently he fell from the wagon on his face into a soft mud hole and was run over by both of the wagon wheels. There was a black and blue line across his back. The doctor thought one of his ribs might be broken. Carlton soon fell asleep and suffered little pain. After two days he was his normal self. Emily was thankful for the mud, which undoubtedly cushioned his fall and probably saved his life.

Emily was so overburdened with work it seemed as if she would sink, but she was assured of the promise, "the bruised reed He will not break." (Isaiah 42:3) She was without a girl to help her again, and as she sought out Ida, whom she had had before, she

---

[103] May 18, 1872.
[104] July 14, 1872.

discovered two weeks before she had run off with a married man, probably back to Jamaica. Emily was heart sick as she thought of all that had been done to try and train Ida in the truths of Christ and encourage her to follow Him.

When the time came for the American Board of Commissioners of Foreign Missions' annual meeting in New Haven, Emily's mother offered to take the children and have them stay with her. Emily welcomed the needed rest and accepted the offer. After depositing the children in Salisbury, Emily and Milton left for South Hadley, where they visited Mt. Holyoke just as evening devotions were begun. Three of Emily's classmates were now instructors at the school; only one of her instructors, Miss Shattuck, remained, "beautiful with rosy cheeks and snowy curls of her fifty years, she stands as an enthusiast in her work, making the natural sciences to gleam out of their darkest corners, and reveal their most hidden secrets."[105] After a most pleasant evening and breakfast at the school, they procured a team and went to Amherst, where Milton could visit the Appleton Cabinet, which contained an Ichnological collection, a zoological collection, and a museum of Indian relics. Arriving in New Haven, they stayed with Maggie Magill, Emily's roommate from Mt. Holyoke. The meetings of the A.B.C.F.M. were spiritually rich. The Friday afternoon after the meeting they visited West Rock:

> We rambled about in the woods, threw stones in the river, ate barberries, drank cider at the mill where it was made and finally came home in the dusk of the evening on the horse cars feeling more rested after our rigorous mountain climbing than we had been all the week.

They enjoyed walking around Yale college, then Monday afternoon visited Savin Rock in West Haven:

---

[105] October 27, 1872

where we had a fine view of the Sound. It was high tide, and there was wind enough so that the white caps were many and beautiful. To sit on the high rocks and see and hear the waves dashing upon them was romance, poetry, fascinating, delight. I took a breath of intense satisfaction feeling that the vision would last for many days, and as we turned our backs upon the scene I folded it up and laid it away to be brought out on rainy and gloomy days, and talked over with the children.[106]

Monday evening they took a boat for New York, waking up in the city. They walked throughout Central Park, ate peach pie in a lovely arbor, then chartered an open carriage to ride for miles and miles through the loveliest scenery. There were classmates to visit in the next few days, and an evening at the opera. When they returned to Salisbury, the little folks were well and glad to see them: "This was of course to the Mother heart the crowning moment of the journey."

It seemed the church in Orwell had grown cold, but during the annual week of prayer at the beginning of 1873, many came to Christ and others renewed their walk with the Savior. One who first stood for Christ was Julia Cofren. She came from a family of unbelievers, and it was difficult for her to stand alone, "if anyone can be said to stand alone who stands with Christ." One evening, coming out of the meeting, Julia grasped Emily's hand, and with tears streaming down her cheeks, she asked Emily to help her love for Christ, since she didn't have any encouragement among her family. Her husband, who had been praying for her conversion, was traveling on business at the time. The Church's renewal continued in ensuing months, with many who had grown cold returning to Christ as their first love, and others rejoicing to know Christ for the first time. Several young men were beginning to follow Jesus, prodigals who had known Christ in their childhood

---

[106] October 27, 1872.

returning to their faith. Milton personally counseled many in their faith, and in the spring Claudie, at age eleven, was received into membership of the church.

During the summer Claudie spent three months at his Grandfather Spencer's helping with some of the farm work. When Milton's mother came for a two week visit, she was extremely helpful in helping with the sewing and making the boys' winter suits. Other friends and relatives came and stayed for various lengths of time. Six year old Carlton had another accident. He went out with Claude and Willie to visit some panoramic slides of the Holy Land. Rushing home, he stumbled and fell, and two other "heedless boys" on a horse trampled on him. It was a night of horror when little Carlton was brought home all covered with blood. Thankfully, the wound was not dangerous. The wound was sewn up with several stitches, and he fully recovered. Yet, it gave Emily a terrible shock, "but such are a Mother's cares and burdens."[107]

Finding help with her housework and in the kitchen was frequently difficult. Emily's Mt. Holyoke roommate, Matilda Magill, suggested she hire an orphan from the orphanage in New Haven. When Lizzie came, she was "homely, awkward and careless but good tempered and stored with many pretty children's songs."[108] The girl was totally unaccustomed to housework, and Emily needed much patience in bearing with her, but she improved and became a great help: "I felt when she came that the finger of God was in it, and I hope that I shall have no reason hereafter to think otherwise."

---

[107] August 27, 1873.
[108] February 15, 1874.

December 2, 1873, Herbert Allen brought the number of Emily's children to five. Herbert was a fussy baby, and the care of her children continued to weigh heavily upon Emily:

> The older children, who are all boys, each one with a strong individuality of his own, give us more care and anxiety than the younger ones. Claude wants to domineer and Willie won't be one of his subjects. He is a restless, uncomfortable child, always ready to cry out every time any one comes near him…Carlton is quick tempered and flashes up at very slight provocation but is easily soothed and made to see his folly when he is ready to repeat the same, repentance and all. Each one of these boys would be a paragon if taken alone, but all together there is jarring and discord enough to test the paternal government right seriously….When I look around upon this large group of children and think that I am in some sense responsible for their training and development, and that I hold their future very much in my own hands, I realize that the work before me is stupendous. There is no longer any chance to think of literary work, my hands are full, <u>so full</u> that the work drops out of them, spilling over on every side, and I say to myself consolingly, when I think of the half dozen Sabbath School books I was to have written, "Never doubt but you are doing the highest and holiest work woman was ever called upon to do."[109]

Amidst all the cares, Emily had a calm, undercurrent of <u>peace</u>. She hoped that "the same mind which was in the Lord Jesus" was developing in her.[110] She wanted to "be <u>willing</u> not to be ministered unto, but to minister, willing to serve my day and generation in the same spirit in which He served His."

---

[109] March 8, 1874.
[110] April 5, 1874. Philippians 2:1-5; Matthew 20:28.

In September 1874, thirteen year old Claudie received an appointment to be a messenger for the Vermont House of Representatives in Montpelier. He boarded with Col. Hopkins, who spoke of Claudie as "modest, honest, and hearty," and the "pet of the family." When Milton had to go to Norwich, Vermont, he stopped at Montpelier to see Claude and was very gratified at the esteem in which he was held. In fact, Milton was treated with special attention because he was Claude's father! Mr. Nichols, the Secretary of State told him, "He had not been here three days before I knew he had a good Mother…I did not know anything about his father, but I knew he had a good Mother." One of the representatives pronounced Claude, "the smartest boy in Montpelier." When Emily recorded this in her diary, she wrote,

> The best of it all is Claude does not seem to have his head turned in the least by all this flattery, seems pleased and encouraged to merit a good opinion, but does not feel unduly elated by it. Perhaps the fact of my writing this all down argues a contrary effect upon the Mother, but I trust this is not so. It would be unnatural not to rejoice in the first fruit of a training so careful and tender as he has received, and not take it as a hopeful omen of the good he may accomplish in years to come.[111]

With Claude away, Willie took on more responsibilities at home. Over the summer he earned twelve dollars driving cows to pasture, and he was doing well in school. He had a bent for mechanics and developed "many ingenious devices which keep his mind pure and sweet and occupy his leisure moments in a way to drive out low and groveling thoughts." Carlton had a sunny disposition and "in spite of his numberless bumps and bruises he is sure to come out right side up and with a broad grin on his face."

---

[111] November 22, 1874.

In 1875, about the middle of January, the church came in a body and paid Milton and Emily a visit, bringing with them their own entertainment and food. Some made private gifts, amounting to $17: "It was a pleasant occasion, full of love and good cheer." The winter was filled with several "sociables," including surprise visits from Milton and Emily's Sabbath School classes. There were also several sugaring parties, where friends would visit as the maple sap was boiled until the sugars concentrated into syrup. A more sorrowful gathering on February 14, was the funeral of Ellen, wife of Emily's brother Orrin. In her last illness, Ellen eagerly anticipated Heaven, knowing she would want to write her family and tell them what a good time she was having! If Orrin could have had his choice, he would have gone with her, but he had duties claiming him in Salisbury. Emily reflected that after six weeks,

> No letters came back from the silent land into which she has gone and the months and years will go by and we shall never, never hear. If we could only hear from her once in a while it would not be so bad. If we could know from her lips that the angelic convoy which she thought she saw about her bed was a reality, and that she had entered the Father's house…it seems as if it would make us willing to wait, as if it would greatly shorten the time till we too are called hence. But then there would be less faith and less need of faith on our part. Moses and the Prophets we have already, yea and God's own Son has pledged his word to the truth of revelation, "If it were not so I would have told you, I go to prepare a place for you." If we believe not such witnesses, we do not deserve to be assured by our beloved dead.[112]

May 10, Emily's family and friends from Orwell attended the Centennial celebrations at Ticonderoga, commemorating Ethan

---

[112] March 14, 1875. Luke 16:29; John 14:2.

Allen's capture of the fort from the British one hundred years previous. Joseph Cook was the orator of the day and gave a moving presentation. Cook had grown up near Ticonderoga and as a young man interviewed many of the older people in the area who were familiar with Ticonderoga's history, especially during the Revolution. His *Sketches of Ticonderoga* remains an important history of the region. Cook had graduated from Harvard, then studied at Andover in preparation for becoming a Congregational minister. His oratorical skills were legendary, and he became a lecturer on Christianity, morals, and history throughout the United States and indeed the world.[113] He had spoken at Milton's church a number of times and was friends with Emily and Milton. When he delivered a course of lectures at Mount Holyoke, he mentioned several Mount Holyoke alumnae he had met in his many travels, but the highest praise he gave to Emily.[114] Shortly after the Ticonderoga Centennial, Milton went to the Bunker Hill Centennial outside Boston. Milton's great, great uncle Ephraim Kirby had fought at the battle of Bunker Hill, and one of his ancestors, Gamaliel Leonard, was among the militia in Roxbury, which was bombarded before the fighting of Bunker Hill. Milton recalled growing up in Middlebury and hearing stories about the Revolutionary War and his relatives' roles recounted in the long winter evenings.

When August came, Emily and Milton again went to the commencement exercises in Middlebury. Claude had been working in a store in Bristol during the summer, and he joined the family and friends in this annual reunion. Besides the college activities, they, with friends from Orwell and beyond, were able to visit Whiteface and Lake Placid in New York. Emily had never actually

---

[113] Frederick G. Bascom, "Joseph Cook and Ticonderoga," *New York History*, Vol. 15, No.1, January 1934, 43-49.
[114] "Letters of the Class of '58", 1876, 17. Mount Holyoke Archives.

been among the Adirondacks and was excited about the prospect. She found the Ausable Chasm a moving sight:

> The [Ausable] river wears its deep channel through the rocks some four or five miles in all, and is characterized all the way by wondrous beauty. From lofty heights above you look down to see it break in numerous cascades one above another, sometimes forming a double horseshoe in its fall, and again tumbling at random over its rocky bed. At length you look down and behold it hemmed in by rocky barriers and think you have reached an end of the wonders, but you follow on and turning a sharp corner find it stretching away as before giving itself up to new gambols with the wind and rocks.[115]

Emily was sorry there was no time to take a boat and ride over the rapids.

The next morning they started for Whiteface, which was a six mile ascent. They rode horses the first two miles then walked the rest:

> The ascent was easy considering that the mountain was 5000 feet high, and we made the distance in about 4 hours, reaching the summit at half past ten. We were amply rewarded for all the long toilsome way when we reached the glorious lookout at the top. The vision is unobstructed in every direction, as no trees grow near the summit. The clouds hung low making long shadows on the earth. And we could not see as far with the naked eye as on some clearer days…

They stayed on the summit two hours, eating a lunch of fried potatoes and doughnuts while being refreshed by the scenery. Emily was pleased she "had no trouble in making the descent as fast as 'his reverence' wished, often calling out to him to clear the track."

That evening, Emily had her first experience of camping out:

---

[115] August 3, 1875.

five feminine frames so snugly dispersed that neither one could move without moving the other four…there was now and then an awaking consciousness of aching hips and when morning dawned we were only too glad to quit our recumbent position and resume our places around the camp fire.

The following evening, after a ride across the lake, Emily described as "the gayest evening of my life." Sitting around the campfire, the companions sang, told stories, played games, and had a marvelous time. That evening Emily slept in a hammock, "with no covering between me and the stars."

Often times Emily felt that sewing clothes and knitting stockings for the family could consume all of her time, not to mention the general housework and keeping "a sharp lookout to the morals of my children."[116] In May of 1876, everyone in the family had Scarlet Fever, beginning with Claude. Milton's case was not as bad as the rest, for he had had the disease as a child. Neighbors and friends were very kind in bringing food and helping to care for the family. There were a number of deaths in the community from the disease, and Emily was thankful when they had all weathered the storm.

Emily was also very active in community and church affairs. As she reported to her Mount Holyoke sisters:

There is enough to occupy hands and heart at home, but outside, is the beloved Woman's Board [of Missions] to be planned for and prayed for, a children's missionary meeting to be promptly attended every month, a sewing society to be encouraged, and a reading circle to be desired, besides the numberless calls and visits that belong to social life.[117]

Emily had carefully planned for the young people's missions group. 52 youngsters attended the first meeting in the parsonage.

---

[116] November 21, 1875.
[117] "Letters to the Class of '58", 1876, 16, Mount Holyoke Archives.

They chose officers and a name for their group – the Orwell Evergreens. Emily trusted "their verdure will continue right on forever."[118] They recited the 24th Psalm together, sang some hymns, and repeated the Lord's Prayer before reading some articles about missionary work around the world. The Orwell Evergreens met monthly, and the organization flourished. The young people raised funds and sent them to Henry Perry, a missionary in Sivas, Turkey. Perry's sister, Sarah Ann Porter, was a classmate of Emily's at Mount Holyoke, and the two had kept in contact.

August always had a special week of anniversaries: Emily's brother Nathaniel died of his Civil War wounds August 20; Willie was born on August 18, Carlton on August 15; and Emily and Milton were married on August 16. In 1876, Emily looked back over seventeen years of marriage and wrote,

I know the mountain tops and the ravines and bridgeless chasms in my life. The pleasant valleys, and sheltering woods, the cliffs and lanes and hedgerows; and as I look back upon it glad and grateful I pronounce it a happy life. For though I have had much of rich and keen enjoyment, I have learned to be happy without some things which I deemed essential to my happiness and instead of pining for a coveted thing just beyond my reach, I have learned to take the things that came naturally and legitimately and be happy in their enjoyment. I do not say this has been done without many a silent pang and wrench but I say nevertheless that it has been done. I suppose when I was married I believed my husband to be little short of perfection, he was my hero, my ideal. I now know him to be larger, fuller, and stronger in all moral proportions than he then was, more worthy the love of any cultivated and high-minded woman, so that if I was willing then to try the experiment of life together, I

---

[118] June 4, 1876.

should now be more than willing to share with him the richness and the remnant of my days.[119]

In September, Emily and Milton joined Milton's sister Martha Knapp and friends from Orwell in visiting the Centennial Exposition in Philadelphia.[120] Philadelphia was chosen as the site of this world fair in part because here the Declaration of Independence had been approved and signed one hundred years earlier. The group spent nine days in Philadelphia, visiting the numerous exhibits as well as Independence Hall and Carpenters Hall. The Main Building of the Exhibition was the largest building in the world at that time, covering 21.5 acres. Exhibits from the United States were placed in the center of the building, with foreign exhibits arranged around it, depending on the country's distance from the United States. Emily was most interested in the exhibit of minerals and precious stones, though she also noted the "silverware, porcelain, laces, furs, embroidery, lacquered ware, bronzes carpets, ...and everywhere the taste displayed in the arrangement of articles so that they should show to their best possible advantage."[121]

Machinery Hall included exhibits on machinery and industry, with the United States taking up two-thirds of the exhibit space. Most impressive was the Corliss Centennial Steam Engine, which ran power to all the building's machinery as well as other buildings at the Exhibition. There were looms for weaving Brussels carpet and tapestry as well as exhibits on sewing machines, wood carving saws, and the making of wall paper, newspapers, glassware, and so

---

[119] August 16, 1876.
[120] Emily doesn't actually say which of Milton's sisters attended the Exhibition with them, but since Rev. Winchester is not mentioned as present, the assumption is that the sister was Martha Knapp rather than Mary Catherine Winchester.
[121] October 11, 1876.

much more. The Agricultural Hall had a refrigerator which kept meat fresh for a month!

September and October were the peak months of the Exhibition, with almost 100,000 people a day attending. On several days, Emily, Milton, and Martha rose early to go to the Art Gallery in Memorial Hall before the crowds gathered. Both Milton and Martha, as well as Milton's sister Mary, were painters, and they took advantage of the opportunity to visit some of the renowned art brought from Europe for the Exhibition. Emily particularly liked the landscape paintings of the American west by Albert Bierstadt.

After nine days in Philadelphia, they went to visit friends and sites in Washington, D.C. They toured the Capitol building and saw the Senate Chambers, Representative Hall and paintings of the nation's early history. They went to the highest point of the Dome possible and spent almost an hour studying the different scenes before them – the Potomac, the White House, Patent Office, Lincoln Memorial, and more. They then visited Mt. Vernon, the home of George Washington. Emily found that "a spirit of awe pervades the place, a beautiful peaceful home for a retired statesman worthy of his noble life, and congenial to his refined taste."

On Sunday they attended the Methodist Episcopal Church and heard Dr. John Phillip Newman, who had been chaplain of the United States Senate for several years. Cousins living in Washington took Emily and Milton around to visit other sites later in the week: the Smithsonian, the White House, the new War and Navy Departments, Arlington, the Government Printing Office, and the Corcoran Art Gallery.

One evening they attended a prayer meeting of black Christians. Emily was somewhat familiar with black culture from reading Harriet Beecher Stowe's *Uncle Tom's Cabin*, but she was not prepared for anything quite so exciting. They would shout and clap their hands and speak so rapidly and catch their breath that we could hardly distinguish a word. In the next room they would get right down on the floor and roll over and over.

Their weeks of travel were filled with numerous memorable sites, people, and places, but for Emily, "There was no happier moment in all my journey than that in which I clasped the dear children once again and thanked God for guarding them so tenderly."

Chapter 4 – Educators in Middlebury and Manchester

"Now these are the commandments, the statutes, and the judgments…And thou shalt teach them diligently unto thy children and shall talk of them when thou sittest in the house, and when thou walkest by the way, when thou liest down, and when thou resist up." Deuteronomy 6:1, 7

Emily had a sympathetic nature and was drawn to praying and helping those in need, though she did remark that "This parish work is a great drain on one's sympathies. One needs to have a very large heart to take it all in."[122] One week there was Judge Bollin, "one of our oldest and respected citizens" at the point of death, a wedding of two well-suited young-people, and, saddest of all, a bride of five years facing cancer. Julia Cofren had only recently come to Christ. For two years she had some problem with her knee. The doctors had found it was cancer in the bone and her leg was to be amputated. Julia bore the surgery with courage and a cheerful spirit. Emily reflected,

How certain it is that we can never lay our hand upon any portion of earthly happiness however small, and claim it as

---

[122] September 21, 1877.

ours, the moth eats and the rust corrupts, and nothing is more certain than that trial in some form will be our portion.[123]

She reflected too on the passing of her relative Harriet Ann Spencer, who had suffered for all the twenty-five years Emily had known her, unable to speak above a whisper, yet a beautiful Christian. She had no income, was an expense to her relatives and friends for years, but never a burden to them. She was rich toward God "with a kind of riches the Astor's and the Rothschilds never knew." She could do little,

> But to her was appointed that more rare and difficult service which the church and the world both need, of showing the power of the Christian faith to sustain in seasons of affliction, and this she did so bravely, patiently, resignedly, triumphantly that it was good to know that human nature <u>could</u> be so refined and wrought upon. It is a blessed thing to see one wearing the mantle of patience under trials for thirty or forty years, but it is a much more glorious thing to wear it for sixty years, and so wear it that at the end of that time it can be laid down in exchange for a crown.[124]

1878 marked the 20th anniversary of Emily's graduation from Mt. Holyoke. She excitedly looked forward to the reunion in June, and took eight year old Maude with her. Emily had been asked to write an essay for the class meeting, and she worked on it at odd times of the day. Before leaving, she had Milton read it. He was not impressed, saying "my forte was not this kind of writing, I was off my beat, and much more of the same import."[125] There was not time to rewrite, and Emily had to make the best of it. She was anxious when it came time to deliver her essay to her classmates,

---

[123] September 26, 1877. Matthew 6:19-20.
[124] October 14, 1877.
[125] July 13, 1878

yet it was very well received, and they voted to have it read again at their 25th reunion.

Back at home, Emily continued to prepare Claude for college, tutoring him in his Latin and Greek. He would be attending College in the fall. The family acquired a piano, and Claude and Maude began taking piano lessons.

Yet, sorrowful changes were coming to Emily. Her father, at 87, was increasingly feeble. Emily went and spent several days with him for a number of weeks before he was called to his heavenly home, January 22, 1879. His faith was strong throughout his weakened state. The pastor's funeral sermon was from Revelation 14:13, "Blessed are the dead who die in the Lord from now on." 'Blessed indeed,' says the Spirit, 'that they may rest from their labors, for their deeds follow them!'"

Some deacons approached Milton and said there was some dissatisfaction in the parish and many desired a change of pastors. They could give no specific cause for complaint, but in other conversations some thought the preaching too plain; others thought there was not enough visitation. Some of the wealthier members felt neglected. Milton resigned after communion services on New Year's Day 1879. Many were surprised by the move, and a meeting was called to consider the resignation. The Council voted 19 to accept and 26 to refuse the resignation. The opposition continued to refuse to give any specific complaints against Milton. And so, Milton remained pastor at Orwell.

When the railroads advertised some inexpensive rates to Montreal (for $2.50) and Quebec (for $4.50) in the fall, the Severances, with five others from the Orwell church, decided to take advantage of the rates and make the trip. For these New England Puritans, exposure to practices of the Catholic Church was most interesting. They began with a visit to Notre Dame in Montreal, which they were told imitated St. Peter's at Rome: "The statues, and paintings, the confessionals, the skull bones, and the keys of St. Peter, and the long list of Romish mummeries, each had a kind of fascination for us, as things of which we had heard much and seen little."[126]

After visiting Notre Dame, they hired guides and carriages to take them around the city. Their first stop was the Grey Nunnery. There they saw a newborn baby in a crib, who had been left for the nuns to care for, classes of little boys, older boys, and another room with sick old ladies. Emily conceded there was much good being done there. In the afternoon they drove around the terraced side of the mountain:

The afternoon was lovely. The sun's mild rays fell upon the bright October tints, and here and there patches of scarlet bloom, untouched by frost, hinted at late and kindly warmth in the Queen's dominions. We could have wished the ride prolonged indefinitely, the conditions of enjoyment were so nearly fulfilled…

In the early evening they stopped at the Jesuit Church, where the organist was playing and the Jesuit students singing. Though nothing in Notre Dame appealed to her, at the Jesuit Church, with the classic paintings frescoed on the wall, Emily easily could have fallen to her knees in worship.

During the night they took a steamboat from Montreal to Quebec. In the morning they awakened to see the Heights of Abraham from the deck. The history of the battle upon the Heights, in which the British James Wolfe defeated the French Montcalm, and an entire continent changed hands, was described as they stood upon the deck. Touring the city they first visited St. John's Cathedral, much inferior to Montreal's Notre Dame. There were several interesting paintings, such as the one of the Crucifixion by

---

[126] November 8, 1879

Van Dyck. The Seminary chapel was said to contain the finest collection of religious paintings in America. The tourists were shown the bones of St. Clement in one of the shrines. Emily thought, "Saintship is undoubtedly a good thing, but when it comes to bones we could not have sworn that these did not belong to some lesser luminary!" They were also shown priestly robes of gold and silver, with diamonds, emeralds and rubies.

At the Ursuline Convent there were tolerable paintings. One side of the Chapel was open lattice work, where the nuns were permitted to stand and look while services were held in the chapel. In the reception room they saw a nun dressed in black conversing through an iron grate with two callers. This was the nearest approach to the outside world the nuns had. "Tired and sick of popish mummeries," the tourists took carriages for the Falls of Montmorency. Returning to the ship, they enjoyed a moonlight evening on the deck, as a violinist and harpist played melodiously. It was a nice way to conclude Emily's first journey into a foreign land.

1880 began with the week of prayer, which awakened many to their need for Christ. As there was deep interest in spiritual things, an evangelist was invited to assist in the meetings. Francis Eleanor Townsley, a Baptist evangelist, held meetings for two weeks in March. Emily found Miss Townsley

> a woman of unusual wisdom and tact combined with common sense and consecration. She did us all good…The church was much refreshed and personal work was followed by good success. More than forty persons gave expression to a purpose to live for Christ.[127]

The young people's weekly meeting flourished, and Emily thought "the condition of the Church has never been more promising since

---

[127] May 16, 1880.

we came here." When Emily conducted the young people's meeting, there were about fifty present, and "there was great freedom in song and prayer and remark." One man said "it was the best meeting he had ever attended in the town of Orwell." Emily noted, "Only those who know the anxieties of a pastor's family in leading souls to Christ can truly realize the joy we feel in welcoming these lambs of the flock to a place within the fold."

Though the church work flourished, Milton and Emily were uneasy because of the dissatisfaction some had earlier expressed about the ministry. When an offer came from Middlebury College for Milton to act as their agent for collecting funds for a year, they considered the offer Providential. It would be difficult to separate from so many dear friends, but the Lord's direction seemed clear. Milton resigned the first Sabbath in August 1880.

At their August meeting, the Orwell Evergreens held a picnic at Sunset Lake. Emily read an original poem she had written for them, then they surprised her by presenting her an envelope with $20.35. Howard Royce made the presentation:

> Mrs. Severance, We over whom you have expended your good influences for the past few years, who have been brought together and become more closely united by your efforts in our behalf, wish to return our gratitude to you who have sought to lead us in the path of light and truth, and present a slight token of our affection and esteem in the form of this simple gift, and the best wishes as you go forth to your labor in other fields of the Orwell Evergreens.[128]

After the formal meeting, tables were spread with an ample feast. There was "boating on the lake, singing in the woods, swinging in the hammocks, games and merriment and in the quiet of the evening the company dispersed."

---

[128] March 10, 1881.

At the end of August the church held a farewell gathering at the parsonage. There were appreciative words spoken of both Milton and Emily. A clerical brother of one of the parishioners, visiting from out of town, warned that there would not be another pastor's wife who would bring "such voluminous self-sacrificing labor....I forewarn you not to expect it. I entreat you not to exact it." To Emily, having to leave the parsonage was akin to the first parents leaving the Garden of Eden. Yet, she had no doubts that this was the right thing to do and that God was leading them in His Providence. Emily and Milton had spent twelve years in Orwell. Two of the children were born there, and three had united with the church there. Sabbath by Sabbath, Emily had taught her class of young ladies. Here were many pleasant and sacred memories.

Middlebury College had found itself in financial straits and hired Milton to collect $100,000 from donors. Knowing that their stay in Middlebury would be temporary, Milton and Emily rented a large house during their stay there. Visits and letters from friends in Orwell made the adjustment to their new home easier. On a very cold New Year's day 1881, forty of the Orwell Evergreens even came and visited, bringing their own food and entertainment. Emily was delighted to see them and enjoyed one of the happiest New Year's in memory.

Living in Middlebury provided excellent educational opportunities for Claude, who began college in Middlebury the fall of 1880, and Willie, who entered in the fall of 1881. Emily recognized the Lord's provision for them in both great and small things. As clothes were wearing thin, Emily decided she needed a good dress, and decided upon a summer silk from Wanamaker's Department store in Philadelphia. Her order was returned saying the piece was gone, and there was nothing similar. She then sent to Aunt Martha Severance in New York, to see if she could find something similar. Soon Emily received a letter saying "the dress was purchased and paid for, and was coming <u>as a present</u> from her and Asahel." Emily knew the Lord had put this on their heart to do this:

> I shall prize it beyond any poor estimate of dollars and cents as a pledge of the loving memory in which Christ holds us, caring for our wants, interested in all our comforts, granting needed supplies even for our temporal wants. We are not rich, we have staggered under a burden of debt for years, a burden which is no yet lifted, the education of the children is expensive, and our obligations come in upon us like a flood, and when the clothing wears out so rapidly, and the flour barrels grow empty so soon, it needs real courage to stand boldly and face the music! Then when we grow a little despondent, a gift like this of the dress or even a much smaller one comes with such a delightful assurance that Jesus knows all about it. That He is looking on an interested observer all the while, and that He is engaged to help us, that He is rich and <u>will</u> help us, that He will not suffer us to be much straitened even in temporal things, that the struggle shall end in victory though years must first intervene – all these belong to the joys of the Christian believer for which I am grateful.[129]

The future was uncertain as Milton completed his year as a financial agent for the College, successfully raising the funds required to pay off the College debts. The family remained in Middlebury, as Milton supplied pulpits in surrounding villages. They began to build a house for themselves, moving into an old tenement until the house was complete. It seemed almost unreal to Emily that they would actually have a house of their own:

> …it does not seem at all as if I should ever be permitted to occupy it, so I live on enjoying each day as it comes with very little thought or care for the future remembering the good hand of my God that has been upon me for good all the way and

---

[129] June 19, 1881.

trusting that where I cannot see the way He will lead safely on.[130]

While the house was being built, Milton was offered the position as Principal of Burr and Burton Seminary in Manchester, Vermont. Emily wept and prayed over the decision with Milton. They both wanted to do whatever the Lord wanted them to do, but were they to turn aside from pastoral work? It finally was decided to take the position. Renters were found for the house they had been building, which would be a good home for Emily and Milton in their declining years. Before the move to Manchester, Emily's eighty year old mother came to live with them, leaving her home in Salisbury of fifty years. Emily hoped they would be able to make her happy in their new home.

The first school term at Burr and Burton there were ninety students with three teachers in the upper level, Emily and Milton being two of them! Each had six recitations per day. Through overwork, Milton "broke down with Rheumatism," and then the other teachers had to assume some of his classes as well! Emily especially noted several "crazy girls" in that first year. Fanny Sykes was a tall, graceful girl who could be agreeable, but was deceitful and untruthful. Repeatedly she confessed her faults with tears, then went out and mocked her repentance. One day she even knelt and prayed with Milton and Emily, saying she wanted to be a Christian. The next day she told an outrageous falsehood, revealing her unabashed hypocrisy. Emily hoped and prayed for a thoroughly Christian atmosphere at the school, but feared it was not so. Many of the students were day students, not boarders, and passed out of their influence after school hours.

Emily looked forward enthusiastically to her 25th class reunion at Mount Holyoke. It was a wonderful time of meeting friends,

---

[130] September 18, 1881.

hearing college compositions, and attending concerts. Each person gave a brief report of her history since her graduation, and the ladies alternated laughing and crying together. Emily later wrote, "Hour by hour the characters of these women shone forth as we sat together and moment by moment they became more precious to me, until I felt as never before that it was an honor and a blessing to be of their number."[131] Emily read the poem she had written, which was later printed:

Retrospection

I sing a wondrous morning long ago,
Summer's fresh verdure, and the rapid flow
Of streamlets hastening to find the sea;
Melodious songsters filling bush and tree;
Sunshine on all the hills, with light and shade
Weaving her tapestries, of warmth and color made,
The incense breathing flowers, the dew
Shaking her jeweled fingers as they grew;
Such sights and sounds together wrought to form
The wondrous beauty of that perfect morn.

Who can forget – although 'tis long ago –
For memory serves us though the pulse grows slow –
The parting with our Alma Mater here
Whose presence day by day we held more dear,
The daughters eager with youth's restlessness
Once more her smile to win, her fond caress,
And seek mild fluctuating smiles and tears
Her benedictions for the future years.

"Go," said the mother, as she laid her hand
On each bowed head among that reverent band,
The world needs helpers, to her workshops go,

---

[131] June 24, 1883.

Her anvils wait you, and her forges glow;
Put to the test the wisdom you have gained,
Reach upward to the heights yet unattained,
The storm and calm life's discipline will bring
And Providence apply her chiseling;
I presage nought of ill on morn like this,
But strokes like these you may not, must not miss.

They took their journey and the years rolled on.
Their paths lay far asunder, toward the dawn
One sought her place of work on the far land
Of the celestials, where the scorching sand
Blistered her tired feet uplifting high
The standard of the Cross in orient sky.
Some on the far Pacific slopes were blest,
And some in sunny Southern homes found rest,
Some in the freshness of their young life's love,
Turned from earth's charms to the glad heavens above;
Some walked earth's highways wearily in pain,
And sorrow shrouded some with purpose plain;
Fortune on some bestowed her favors bland,
And Fame sent praise of some throughout the land;
But more in humble homes made life a joy,
Their Master's work for them their best employ.

And so the years swept on, sweet peaceful years,
Life had its harvest rich with joys and tears,
Then burst the thunder, sudden awful, grand,
And son and sire for his imperiled land
Went forth to combat with the power of ill,
And ceased not from the bloody contest till
The clanking chains of servitude no more
Disturbed the listening ear from shore to shore,

103

And the sweet English of our mother tongue
Uttered no bondman's tales from terror wrung.
In the grand issue mothers had their share,
And daughters found relief in grateful prayers,
And all men hailed the year of glad release,
As the true reign of righteousness and peace.

The sands drop in the hour glass, the soft glow
Of morning is no longer, and we know
As we stand scorched in the meridian sun,
That life, for us, is more than half way done;
Once more to us the sheltering mother calls
And opens wide the unforgotten halls,
To the returning pilgrims, who from far
On dusty highways, mid the din and jar
Of life, have heard the summons and have come
To warm themselves and rest once more at home,
'Neath the mild searchings of the mother's eyes,
Whose questioning glance invokes their meek replies.

Life has been real, and most earnest too,
And earth more lost and fallen than we knew;
We have had struggles and we bear the scars
Of many silent and internal wars,
The things we meant to do are still undone,
The heights we thought to reach yet lure us on,
Yet often from dust and ashes have we brought
Gems of pure luster elsewhere vainly sought,
Our nearest duty we have found each day
A messenger of peace to lead the way,
By glad uplifting to immortal heights,
Where doubts and glooms dissolve in endless light,
And in our work we've found the restful sense

Of loving and eternal Providence.

Too brief the hour for all we have to tell,
Of victories gained, of losses that befell,
We only of the class of Fifty-eight,
A remnant at our mother's threshold wait,
Our comrades gather under milder skies,
And walk serener heights in paradise
We glory in their sweet and sure reward,
And long like them to look upon our Lord,
But time and toil are ours, and duty calls,
We leave once more the well-remembered halls,
And with our faces toward the setting sun,
Await reunion when our work is done.

August 16th was not only the anniversary of the battle of
Bennington and the settlement of Ipswich, Massachusetts, but
Milton and Emily's wedding anniversary. For their 25th
anniversary in 1884, Emily invited to tea a few friends from
Orwell, some family members, and her bridesmaids, in all a group
of about forty. Emily wore her wedding dress with her white satin
slippers for the occasion. Many brought presents, which she had
not expected. Looking back over the years, there were so many of
their wedding party who had gone "to the far country" - Pastor
Barrows and his wife, Emily's father, two groomsmen, as well as
others. These were twenty-five years for which to be thankful:

> The Lord has been wonderfully good to us during all these
> years in which we have lived together. In our little household
> there is no missing link, no vacant chair. We have known but
> little sickness. We have had health and the next greatest
> blessing, a plenty to do.

> Our children have been to us a crown of joy, each one dear in
> its own especial way, and with unflagging industry and

economy has come temporal support so that we do not lack for the comforts and conveniences of life. We have had the joy of welcoming dear children one after another into the Savior's fold, until all but the youngest have solemnly avouched the Lord to be their God. As we look in each other's faces "our eyes are not dim nor is our natural force abated" our hair is not gray, and our teeth have not forsaken us. We feel like pledging ourselves anew to Christian service if He spares us yet longer on the earth.[132]

In 1885, during a period when Burr and Burton was closed for repairs to be made to the buildings, Emily and Milton took a vacation of seventy-seven days to Europe. Three weeks of that time was on the ocean coming and going. Emily later wrote her Mount Holyoke classmates, the journey included

…a glimpse of the English and Scottish lakes, with visits to Sterling, Abbotsford and Edinburgh, then a ride across the country to Stratford on Avon and Kenilworth, nine days in London, three on the Rhine, and twelve in Switzerland. Our seventeen days in Italy included visits to Venice, Florence, Rome, Naples, Vesuvius, Pompeii and Pisa. Scarcely a week was left for France, in which we saw Paris and Versailles, after which we turned our faces homeward. [133]

After Claude's graduation from Middlebury, he joined his parents at Burr and Burton, teaching Greek, German, and Latin. When Willie graduated in 1885, he opened a jewelry store in Manchester. Claude then spent a year in Germany, studying at the University of Goettingen, before going to Hawaii in 1886, to teach at the Oahu College for a year. He then decided to study divinity at

---

[132] August 10, 1884. Deuteronomy 34:7.
[133] Letters to Class of '58, December 12, 1889, Mount Holyoke Archives. In her *Diary*, Emily mentioned she had kept a separate diary during their European trip. That diary could not be found by the author.

Yale, preparatory to becoming a missionary in Japan. Milton and Emily had long felt that Claude should enter Christian ministry, and they were pleased he had come to that understanding himself. Carlton graduated from Middlebury in 1889, and in ensuing years was a journalist for newspapers in Chicago, Denver, Boston, Bennington, and Burlington. Though her children were maturing and beginning careers of their own, Emily seemed busier than ever. The recordings in her diary became sparse and often were separated by years rather than just months. Though not recorded in her diary, Emily most probably attended the Mount Holyoke Semi-Centennial in 1887. Her poem "The Old and New" was printed in *Mount Holyoke Semi-Centennial Celebration.*[134]

Emily approached her 50th birthday with a feeling of dread. It was painful to realize she was an old woman. Yet, Milton's constant love as well as the thoughtfulness of her children and numerous friends lessened the gloom.

During their years in Manchester, Milton provided pulpit supply for numerous churches in the region. One of those, the Congregational Church in Bennington Centre gave him a unanimous call to be their pastor in 1888. Emily and the family came to Bennington in the middle of July. So much of the years in Manchester went unrecorded in Emily's diary. Though this she regretted, yet she did not doubt "that one of the sources of enjoyment in heaven will be the power to overlook our whole course, and see not only how many dangers the Lord has brought us through but also how many He has saved us from altogether."[135]

---

[134] Mrs. Sarah Locke Stowe, ed. *Mt. Holyoke Seminary Semi-Centennial Celebration, 1837-1887.* South Hadley, Massachusetts, 1888, 92-96. See Appendix 1.
[135] February 24, 1889.

Chapter 5 - Bennington Center

"For the Lord is a sun and shield: the Lord will give grace and glory;
no good thing will he withhold from them that walk uprightly."
~Psalm 84:11

The Bennington parsonage had been freshly cleaned and papered, and it was a joy to move into. The people seemed the most lovely Emily had ever met. The parsonage had been a stop on the "Underground Railroad" in pre-Civil War days and bordered the grounds where the Bennington Monument was being built. Commemorating the American victory in the Battle of Bennington in 1777, the cornerstone for the monument had been laid in 1887.

The parsonage was ample enough for Emily to board the five or six private pupils she taught. At one time she had "half dozen young, rolicksome, interesting boys, none of them working together in their studies...which makes it more trying for me, but in many ways it seems to me the happiest year I have known in a long time." The students filled the gap of loneliness Emily felt as her own children moved away. Maude had begun studying at

Wellesley, and only Bertie remained at home. Reflecting on her current state in life, Emily wrote

> And so through rainy days and days of sun, the Lord has brought us as a family to the present hour. Our trust is evermore in Him. I am not grateful enough for the many blessings we have received. I am too anxious like those of old to "take the kingdom of heaven by violence," and my patience has to suffer many and severe strokes of the lash and yet I do believe as firmly as ever that "The Lord God is a sun and shield, he giveth grace and glory, and no good thing will He withhold from them that walk uprightly."[136]

Living across the street from where the Bennington Monument was being erected, Emily and Milton had a daily firsthand view of work on the monument. In November 1889, Milton gave the prayer during the ceremonies marking the placement of the capstone:

> Almighty God, our heavenly Father, we thank Thee for this day, and this rare occasion. We do humbly thank Thee for the victory and the achievement of liberty which this solid structure is intended to commemorate.

> We thank Thee for the spirit of freedom which animated our fathers and led them to throw off the yoke of oppression, and for the spirit of loyalty which has led their sons to lift up their deeds to enduring remembrance.

> We thank Thee, O God, that this great work has been so well planned and so successfully brought on its way to completion and now we pray Thee that *Thy benediction* may rest upon it.

> Here may it stand through all generations, an inspiration and power for good to every oppressed and struggling people.

---

[136] February 24, 1889. Matthew 11:12; Psalm 84:11.

As our children and children's children come to look upon this shaft may the spirit of loyalty to our free institutions rekindle upon them, and the love of liberty take possession of every heart, and unto Thee, O, God, shall be the power and glory forever, and ever. Amen.[137]

In September 1890, Claude was ordained in Newton, Massachusetts. His examination was conducted by Dr. Clark of the A.B.C.F.M.. In the evening the public services were held, with Milton giving the ordination prayer. Claude was so happy at his approaching work in Japan, though the approaching separation was difficult for Emily and Milton:

> The night before he left we had prayers in the dining room as it was cold in the parlor, and after Milton had offered a tender and touching prayer for his preservation in travel, and for his usefulness and success when he should reach Japan, Claude continued and prayed for every member of the household, present and absent, calling each by name, and asking for a special blessing on each one. Next morning he was calm and even cheerful and when the horse was at the door to take him to the depot, he went to the piano and sang, "God be with you till we meet again." He sent back letters and postals all the way to San Francisco, and did all he could to soften our grief.[138]

The Bennington Monument was completed in 1891, and a festive parade and dedication ceremonies were held on August 19. President Benjamin Harrison, the governor, and other dignitaries were present for the event, which also celebrated the Centennial Anniversary of the admission of Vermont as a state. The Sunday before, August 16th, a special service was held in the Old First Church at Bennington Centre, attended by Governor Page and

---

[137] *Bennington Banner*, November 28, 1889.
[138] October 18, 1890.

many prominent members from abroad. The interior of the church was decorated with flags and patriotic emblems. Above the pulpit was a beautiful silk flag with a life-sized Eagle on one side and a Union shield on the other. The pulpit was decorated with a Continental flag of 1775 and the first state flag of Vermont. Milton, whose great, grandfather Abraham Kirby had fought at the Battle of Bennington, delivered the historical sermon, taking for his text Psalm 30:12, "Blessed is the Nation whose God is the Lord and the people whom he hath chosen for his own inheritance."[139] It was a moving address reflecting upon God's Providence from the early Pilgrim settlements through the victory at Bennington leading to the formation of the new nation, while also noting the character of the people, and the importance of the Old First Church as the first church in Vermont.

January 1891, one of Emily's most challenging pupils came to board with her; Tobey Gibbs was thirteen:

> Picked up out of the streets, where he had received most of his education, he was well instructed in its language and manners. He was short, bow legged with a shambling gait, and a self assurance beyond his years. But he had a bright face, and a keen searching eye which showed he was used to shifting for himself. His voice was pleasant and kindly and he invariably attracted the favorable attention of strangers.[140]

Miss H.W. Bourne, possibly a Mount Holyoke alum, was paying for Tobey's board and education with Emily. The day after he came, the other boys boarding with her were horrified at his profane language. Emily told the boys when that occurred to tell Tobey that language was against the rules and he could not stay if he spoke that way. He never was heard to use profanity again. He knew little when he came beside rudimentary arithmetic. Morally,

---

[139] See Appendix 2 for Milton's sermon.
[140] August 16, 1893.

Tobey's character was not strong, and his word could not be trusted. He had a love of tobacco and would "indulge in it on the sly."

The first spring he was with Emily, Tobey attended some evangelistic services at the Y.M.C.A. and said he "became converted." He said he would be a minister, and began selecting scriptures and writing sermons. The one he wrote on the history of Job could have been written by a much older boy. He regularly attended religious services and led young people's meetings on occasion. Yet, he continued secretly smoking and chewing tobacco. When he went to work at a hotel as an office boy, he abandoned going to church, began drinking, and stole funds from his employer. Tobey was with the Severances for two and a half years, and Emily provided him a good education so that he could enter College. Yet, his continued dissipation would not be allowed to continue, and Miss Bourne was ready to cut off any more funds for him. Emily thought Tobey's biography was full of important moral lessons, and even wrote out a few scenes which might be included in such a work.

For a brief time Emily had no student boarders. Maude was in school at Wellesley and Bertie enrolled in the Boston Polytechnic (M.I.T.). Wilbert had a jewelry business in Atlantic City which was not flourishing and came home in December to spend the winter. He worked in Holden's Mill while in Middlebury, then in the spring he went back to Atlantic City to close his business. After two weeks, Emily and Milton received a telegram that Willie was insane. Milton immediately went to bring Willie home, where he soon recovered. After a few weeks, however, he had another attack, and the doctors thought he needed to be sent to Brattleboro for special treatment. Willie was very unhappy in Brattleboro, and came home in August, where he seemed as well as ever. Carlton, in Chicago working as a journalist, was attacked by an assassin and "so severely wounded that his life was despaired of, but a merciful providence raised him up and just before Christmas brought him home."[141] In addition, Milton was sick for five weeks that spring, confined to his bed. Emily went alone to attend Maude's graduation from Wellesley in June, a most joyous occasion.

With so much trauma during the year, Milton and Emily readily accepted an invitation by Professor Shipman to spend time at his summer resort at Bayville on the coast of Maine: "We spent ten happy days, rowing, fishing, lounging, reading, roaming through the woods, etc."[142]

When it came time to write her five year letter for her Mount Holyoke sisters, Emily wrote,

> For the most part life has gone smoothly during the last five years, and either with joy or pain, or care, or triumph, my cup has been always full. I have ceased to expect perfect happiness in this life, and conclude that progress is better. To have enough to do and a heart that is interested in doing the daily duty, ought to suffice for anyone. [143]

Emily described each of her children's employment and then commented on the private pupils she had:

> Aside from household cares, I have spent much time with private pupils. Of these I had five boarding in the family at one time, and have never been very long without two or more. Some of them have been so lovely in character and quick to learn, that it has been a pleasure to help them, while others have brought as much discipline to me as I to them. Parish duties have come in for their share of attention, and my Sunday

---

[141] July 30, 1894.
[142] January 30, 1894.
[143] Emily Augusta Severance to "My Dear Classmates," Bennington, Vermont, February 11, 1895. Mount Holyoke Archives.

School class of young men at a formative age, has required tact
if I would keep them interested.

$400 a year was the price Emily charged for boarding and teaching
her private pupils. Not only was she investing in the lives and
future of these young people, she was adding appreciably to the
family income.

Though Emily had a gift for words and wrote poetry and prose
with elegance, her many responsibilities often prevented her from
writing for the requested publisher. One time she wrote to a Miss
Putnam, who had requested an article for a woman's periodical, to
say that she did not have the time for anything new, and all the
articles at hand were too long for inclusion. She selected from
some old papers a poem, "Whip-poor-will: which had never been
in print and could be used if she chose. If used, Emily requested
the "privilege of correcting the proof sheet."

Whip-poor-will

Strange bird in the twilight Roaming!
What is it you have to tell?
Shrieking judgments through the forest,
Waking echoes in the dell?

Come you as a stern avenger
Through the darkness, lone and chill,
Hunting down thru' ceaseless ages,
The erratic, luckless Will?

Hold your lash in air a moment
Ere the sentence you fulfill,
While you tell us what the crime is
Of the miscreant, poor Will!

Is he murderer of your comrade?
Has he plundered all your store?

Branded as a poor relation,
Has he faithless left your door?

Tell us how your sense of justice
Overmasters pity, till
Scourge and condolence you visit
In a breath, on hapless Will!

Is it true as Redmen tell us
Round their camp-fires in the night.
That you came as solemn phantoms
Bursting from the Realms of light?

And Where'er a home is shadowed
By your dusky presence, there
A devastating angel hastens
To secure a victim fair?

Poise your mottled wings and softly
Smooth your jaunty necklace out
While with wise and prompt replying
You shall dissipate thus doubt!

Strange bird clear the mystery round you!
Be your measure faint or shrill,
And append a biographic
Sketch of persecuted Will!

    In Japan Claude had met a young lady from Ohio also working in Japan as a missionary. Almona Gill and Claude Severance were married July 12, 1892. Claude flourished in evangelistic work in Japan, but Mona's health began to deteriorate to the point where they resigned from the A.B.C.F.M. to return to the States. Claude and Mona returned just in time to enjoy the family gathering at Christmas. Maude came from Groton, where she was teaching. Bert came from Boston, where he had been working in the office of architect J.H. Rinn, who had designed the Bennington

Monument. Carlton came from Boston, where he was a journalist for the *Free Press.* Willie, who had opened a jewelry business in Bennington, was living at home. It had been seven years since the family had all been together, and Emily rejoiced to have them all at the Bennington manse. The Christmas festivities were only the beginning. A few evenings later, Emily and Milton had a reception for Claude and Mona, with about fifty people attending. When, a few weeks later, Claude was invited to give a lecture in Orwell, Emily was delighted to attend. There she enjoyed visiting many old friends she had not seen in nine years.

In 1896, Jean Perry came to Bennington to live with the Severances. Her father was a missionary in Sivas, Turkey, and her mother had died at childbirth. After the Armenian massacres of 1894, Henry Perry sent daughter Jean back to the States for safety, entrusting her to the care of his sister Sarah Porter. Sarah Ann and Emily had been classmates at Mount Holyoke; and when one of Sarah Ann's daughters fell gravely ill, Sarah sent Jean to stay with Emily. The Orwell Evergreens had been supporters of Henry Perry in Sivas, so Emily readily welcomed Jean into the family. Emily's heart ached at the suffering and outrages in Armenia, and she welcomed the opportunity to help a missionary family who had done so much for the afflicted Armenians. She agreed to take Jean for two years, with Henry paying $10 a week board for her. Jean flourished under Emily's care and enjoyed the warmth of family in the Bennington manse.

As the New Year came on January 1, 1897, Emily reflected,

Today we begin on a new Calendar and only the Omnipotent knows what the future has for us as we shall tear from it the fresh pages…. I have had much to be thankful for in the last year, and I do not want to forget that my blessings have outnumbered my sorrows. A shadow of discontent has arisen in the parish which seems to have been already dissipated, but how soon it may return or how serious its portent may be we cannot foretell. We have absolute trust in only one thing. God's promises are sure, and though clouds and darkness are round about us, righteousness and judgment are the habitation of his throne. He is our steadfast friend and even if He turns a deaf ear to our pleading we are sure that in some way He is right, and is still looking out for our good and is always interested in our behalf.

The following month, Milton went to Boston for two weeks to attend the meetings of Dwight L. Moody. During January and February, the evangelist held meetings twice a day, except Saturday, in the Tremont Temple. Some, especially the Unitarians, scorned Moody's unscholarly presentations, but Milton welcomed his clear call to repentance and living a life of righteousness in Christ. Carlton, who was in Boston, accompanied Milton to the meetings. Emily hoped that they would help Carlton form lasting commitments. Frederick Meyer came from London for some of the meetings, and temperance evangelist Francis Murphy held daily meetings as well. Emily noted that "Much good is being done."[144]

In the summer of 1897, when President McKinley was vacationing in Vermont. Senator Redfield Proctor, former Vermont governor and U.S. Secretary of State, invited the President to his estate for a reception and celebration of the Battle of Bennington on August 12. There were fifteen hundred guests, and Emily organized a special children's program to be presented for the President, which he particularly enjoyed. After calls for a speech, President McKinley responded:

Senator Proctor and citizens: It gives me great pleasure to pause for a moment to respond to the welcome which has been given me to Proctor. ... I see here to-night not only the men and the women but the boys and the girls. There is in it all the

---

[144] February 12, 1897. Psalm 97:2; Romans 8:28

suggestions of the family. With the family we are reminded to preserve the purity of the home. I trust you will always preserve the purity of our American homes, for from them comes good citizenship and every good citizen gives glory to our country. I am glad to enjoy, as I am enjoying, the splendid hospitality of your illustrious fellow citizen and Senator. I am very glad to receive from you this evidence of good will, and thank you, and bid you good-night.[145]

Emily's mother had been living with them for seventeen years, since she was eighty. When she was ninety, she had climbed to the top of the newly completed Bennington Monument. She slept well, had a good appetite, had no pain, but her mind was under a cloud. Though physically she remained strong, her memory was fading, and her mind was often confused. Her sight was failing, so she couldn't read the newspapers, and she did not understand them if they were read to her. For some years, she could not dress and undress herself. October 29, she fell down the back stairs with a lighted lamp in her hand. There were no broken bones, but her face and head were badly cut and bruised. Though for days she seemed to be getting stronger, on November 11 she began to noticeably weaken. She no longer recognized anyone. A little before 5 o'clock she was gone. Some days later, Emily wrote the last entry in her diary:

The machinery which had done its work so faithfully for 96 years and nearly 2 months refused to act, and our Mother was with her Savior and her kindred from whom she had been long parted. She was the last of a family of 12 children. A woman of great energy of character capable of great sacrifices. She gave two sons to the service of her country, the youngest of whom died in its defense. She was the most cheerful old person I ever knew. She realized that her faculties were impaired but she

---

[145] *The Vermont Watchman*, August 18, 1897.

never seemed depressed or melancholy, as she often said, she did the best she knew how, and then rested the matter.[146]

She was buried in Salisbury, next to Emily's father who had gone on nearly eighteen years before. Emily was the only blood relative who saw her buried. In the other world, two sons, two daughters, and her husband awaited her. Emily was thankful she was taken without suffering, that there were no broken bones, and that she was not burned in her fall – and that she would not have to endure the cold of another winter. Emily knew "The consolations of our religion are unspeakable in a time like this."

In 1898, newspapers were arousing American interest in the Cubans' war for independence from Spain. Senator Redfield Proctor of Vermont closely advised President McKinley on the U.S. response to Cuban independence. McKinley sent the *USS Maine* to protect U.S. interests in Cuba. When the *USS Maine* exploded and sank in Havana Harbor on February 15, there were loud cries for the United States to go to war over this attack. Senator Proctor, in a speech on the Senate floor on March 17 said war was the only remedy, and on April 25, Congress declared war on Spain. On May 9, Carlton, then thirty, enlisted in the Vermont Volunteers. As he left home, fourteen year old Jean Perry gave him a bag of chestnuts, a thoughtful gesture which touched Carlton.[147] When Emily bade farewell, neither she nor Carlton knew this was the last time they would see each other on earth. Carlton was detailed as a clerk at headquarters and was later stationed at Chickamauga, Georgia. His term of service was a brief one from June 19 through July 18. The U.S. reached an armistice in August.

---

[146] November 21, 1897.
[147] Jean Perry and Maude Severance had a close bond of friendship and kept in touch after both had left the Bennington manse. Sixteen or seventeen years later, Maude renewed the connection between Carlton and Jean. They were married June 5, 1915 in Denver, Colorado. They are the parents of Spencer and the author's husband, Gordon.

Within a few days after Carlton's departure from Bennington, Jean was taken ill with diphtheria. Emily carefully nursed her as one of her own children, but within a week Emily herself took ill with diphtheria. She died after only six days of illness. She was buried in the churchyard of the Old First Church in Bennington, not far from the graves of the Hessian soldiers who had died at the Battle of Bennington over a century before. The newspaper notices and condolences which poured in extolled Emily's many virtues as a teacher, pastor's wife, and loving Christian who lived to serve others.

Senator Proctor told President McKinley about Emily's sudden passing; McKinley had so enjoyed the children's presentation she orchestrated the previous August. McKinley wrote a letter of sympathy to Milton, expressing his admiration for Emily as an "able writer and charming woman."[148]

The Middlebury Register noted that

As a teacher Mrs. Severance had qualities rarely excelled. She sought to inspire her pupils to put conscience into all their work. She taught them to be satisfied with nothing that could be improved. She had a happy faculty of throwing additional light on whatever subject she was endeavoring to explain…She loved knowledge, and she loved to impart it to others. …It was her life to be turning wandering, aimless feet into paths of wisdom and virtue….

She loved the Old First Church, and she loved the people midst of its natural surroundings…Mrs. Severance's intellectual powers and intuitions were of a high order. No person was quicker to interpret the tenderer emotions of human hearts, and none more quick to respond. She was especially gifted in the comprehension of literature. By readiest intuition she got from

---

[148] Note in Emily Augusta Severance's file in the Mount Holyoke Archives.

her reading all that the author had put into it. A well written book was a continual feast to her. She was a great lover of true poetry. The choicest gems of all the great poets were stored in her mind. At one time I think she could recite from memory at least half of Milton's *Paradise Lost.* The most beautiful hymns of all the ages were treasured in her memory to be called up at any time. In the twilight she would sit down with her family and repeat the choicest passages from Tennyson, Longfellow, Whittier, Lowell, and others. She apprehended the beautiful everywhere, whether in nature, in literature, in art, or in character. Her own mind was singularly pure, and wanted to find only purity in others. There was no sham about her, what she seemed to be, she was in reality. She despised everything in character that was not genuine. She abhorred wrongdoing and was ready to visit it with righteous indignation. How her heart bled at thought of the suffering and outrages in Armenia! To right the wrongs of starving Cuba she was willing that her boy should enlist in the army, and put his life in jeopardy in the cause of humanity. She was always willing to make sacrifice for the well-being of fellow men. Mrs. Severance's friendships were…built…on a rock foundation. They were cemented with love and made to stand from youth to age. Something Christian and spiritual with no mixture of cheap and showy tinsel, was wrought in them. Her friends lived in her thought from day to day and from year to year. Her Christian faith was colossal. She conceived of nothing as being too hard for the Lord. Nothing was too hard for her to undertake that she felt the Lord wished her to do. The great work of missions, both at home and abroad, engaged her constant thought. No sacrifice she could make was counted to great for the Lord. She took great delight in organizing mission circles, and in educating the people to the importance of this work in Christ's kingdom. Her work in

Orwell during the twelve years that she dwelt in the parsonage remains a monument to her Christian zeal among that people.

But how shall we close this sketch of a life that was so filled with good works? Mrs. Severance had faults, for she was human. But plane these down to their lowest level, grind out all the flaws that can be detected by the most critical human eye, and there would still be enough left of womanly virtues and graces to make hers a character of rare size and great beauty. There are people that you meet and forget that you had ever seen them. They add nothing to your pleasures. They awaken no interest, stir no emotions. They give you nothing that you can take away. There are others whose presence is like a festival. To spend an hour with them is like sitting at a table from which you rise refreshed and strengthened and able to go on your way rejoicing. Mrs. Severance always had something to give. She was everywhere the true woman, gifted, cultured, appreciative, sympathetic, and endowed with large common sense....[149]

The Middlebury Register also printed a letter Milton received from a friend in Chicago:

My dear friend – I am sore distressed by the sad tidings of your supreme bereavement, and know not how to express the sorrowing sympathy which fills my heart. Among all the excellent women whom it has been my good fortune to know no one has seemed to me to surpass your sainted wife in that admirable and precious combination of qualities which, incapable of definition, we strive vainly to express by the word womanliness. From childhood she was singularly thoughtful,

---

[149] "Emily Augusta Severance" obituary, *The Middlebury Register*, June 17, 1898.

reverent, unselfish, sincere, gentle and sympathetic, and to the generous gifts of nature grace added piety so profound, so all embracing, so divine, that despite her modest reticence, her character shone with saintly splendor. She was the incarnation of the Golden Rule, and her life was an unbroken record of gracious deeds. After a life consecrated to the noblest aims and full of well doing, having already seen the ripening fruitage of her loving toil, and rejoicing in the partial fruitions of her hopes, while yet in the midst of a useful career, she heard her Father's voice and passed peacefully over the dark river and up the shining heights on which forever lingers lovingly the soft splendors of "The light that never was on sea or land." There she awaits our tardier footsteps. Twining the myrtle wreath of her victory over the last enemy with the cypress of the chastened grief of bereaving ones, I join with them in paying a tender tribute to the memory of her who lived wisely, loved fondly, and wrought earnestly and to the full measure of her power.

With all the beautiful words describing Emily's life, character, and works, most fittingly might be added those words of Proverbs 31:

An excellent wife who can find?
    She is far more precious than jewels.
The heart of her husband trusts in her,
    and he will have no lack of gain.
She does him good, and not harm,
    all the days of her life.
She seeks wool and flax,
    and works with willing hands.
She is like the ships of the merchant;
    she brings her food from afar.
She 'rises while it is yet night
    and provides food for her household
    and portions for her maidens....
She dresses herself with strength

and makes her arms strong.
She perceives that her merchandise is profitable.
Her lamp does not go out at night.
She puts her hands to the distaff,
and her hands hold the spindle.
She opens her hand to the poor
and reaches out her hands to the needy.
She is not afraid of snow for her household,
for all her household are clothed in scarlet.
She makes bed coverings for herself,
her clothing is fine linen and purple.
Her husband is known in the gates
when he sits among the elders of the land...
Strength and dignity are her clothing,
and she laughs at the time to come,
She opens her mouth with wisdom,
and the teaching of kindness is on her tongue.
She looks well to the ways of her household
and does not eat the bread of idleness.
Her children rise up and call her blessed;
Her husband also, and he praises her:
"Many women have done excellently,
but you surpass them all."
Charm is deceitful, and beauty is vain,
but a woman who fears the Lord is to be praised.
Give her the fruit of her hands,
And let her works praise her in the gates.

Appendix 1

The Old and the New[150]
Mrs. M.L. Severance, Manchester, VT
(Emily A. Spencer, '58)

In ages past, old chronicles relate,
A cavalcade passed out the Tabard gate;
A monk, a parson, prioress, and friar,
A knight, a clerk, a pardoner, and squire;
Full thirty souls on pilgrimage intent,
Each pledged to tell a story as they went.

But, in the progress of this later day,
Hundreds of devotees are on their way;
Pilgrims alike, but in this motley crowd
No longer knight and friar are allowed,
But maidens, spinsters, madams manifold,
With parsons in the background young and old
Equipped with satchel, bandbox, or umbrel –
Appendages in which the fair excel;
And each, less moderate than the band of old,
Has twenty stories waiting to be told.
If crowned saints can still be thought to know

---

[150] Sarah Locke Stowe, ed. *Mt. Holyoke Seminary Semi-centennial Celebration, 1837-1887*. South Hadley, Massachusetts, 1888. Poem read at the Alumnae Association meeting in 1887.

The honors offered to their shrines below,
To gain the homage of such zealous crowd
A Becket would turn over in his shroud.

Ye drooping elms, upon whose front appears
The grace and beauty of your added years,
We reach our hands to you; no marks of age
Have marred the glory of your heritage
The busy tread of generations gone
Who've sat beneath your shade and journeyed on,
Thinking their thoughts, going their varied ways, -
You keep no record of the bygone days;
You call no roll, you do not even sigh
As long processions yearly pass you by.
We name the names, within our hearts we hold
These trysting places of the days of old,
Ye mountains, and ye sunsets, tint and glow
That overspread the landscape then as now!
Ye all have journeyed with us, and have wrought
More than we know upon the roof of thought.

These classic halls we greet, though now no more
They echo to our footfalls as of yore;
Our pilgrim garb they may not recognize,
Nor read the story moistening in our eyes;
Truant, with half filled baskets we have come
Singing the praises of our early home.
Not the proud sovereign in her coronet,
On whose extended rule no sun has set,
Nor he who, by the Tiber, calmly waits
The willing tribute of unnumbered states,
Can summon a more loyal confidence,
Or gratitude more reverent and intense,

The honors offered to their shrines below,

While vassals gather from two hemispheres
To weave the chaplet for their fifty years.

And ye instructors of the vanished past,
Your bread at morn upon the waters cast
We bring again to you; full oft since then
Has it brought nourishing to famished men,
And like the golden bough Proserpine
Requires of strangers who her realms would see,
Divided oft, the deftly horded store
Has still increased and multiplied the more,

And ye who patient at the helm hold sway
And bear the honors of a later day,
We can your faces with expectant air,
Haply to find familiar features there.
Ah yes! We know you, there is magic now
To drive illusions from a fevered brow,
To know ye once were classmates, sisters, peers,
Our loved companions in the bygone years,
If ye've outstripped us running in life's race
Ye wear your honors with peculiar grace,
And in your gladness on this festal day
We lesser folk rejoice, as well we may.

As travelers in some antique aisle of prayer
Will note the battle flags suspended there,
And pause to murmur 'neath the somber yew,
This waved at Ivry, this at Waterloo,
So, too, our tattered banners placed on high
Tokens of conflict seem, and victory.
These hopeless rents, alas, what tales they tell
Of triumphs gained, or losses that befell!

The Story of Emily

They mark the ashes of extinguished fires,
Of aspirations, longings, dreams, desires;
They speak of struggle and temptation met,
Of folly, indecision, and regret,
Of beacon lights that, often faint and dim,
Led our repentant spirits back to Him
Whose blessings undeserved, day by day,
Spread their white tents at nightfall round our way.
The purposes we formed are unfulfilled;
The plans we cherished, and the hopes that thrilled
Like exhalations of the morning, rose
To mock us with their folly at its close.

Ye sought O teachers of the long ago,
To give us fitting armor, and to show
That in the conflict waged with pride and pelf
The hero of the battle rules himself.
If by one hair's breadth you had failed in this
It had been easier our path to miss.

Ye who now learn the lesson we once learned,
And turn the pages that our fingers turned,
Youth, beauty, grace, a triple diadem
Ye wear, more lustrous than Brazilian gen;
Her phantoms lure you, and her siren's praise.
We glory in the privilege you share –
The opportunity to do and dare.
Fossils we seem to you, whose work is done,
Folded and laid away from air and sun.
But youth is patient, you will not forget
That in these fossils hearts are beating yet;
The cinders smolder in the silent urn,
But stir the embers and the fires will burn.

Appendix 1

Between the greetings in an undertone
We listen for the voices we have known;
To us these halls seem echoing the tread
Of feet that move among the nameless dead,
A rustle as of wings is in the air,
And euthanasias whispered everywhere
The walls are frescoed with the wise, the good,
And all the place becomes a Holyrood.

We check the thought, the hour we would not dim
By selfish thought of saints or seraphim,
May we not hope that in your happier sphere
Some thought is given to work accomplished here?
As she whose loyal soul here prayed and wrought
To rear these walls will send a backward thought,
Will not some richer notes be made to ring
Because of gladness in the songs we sing?
Perish the thought that souls can aught forget!
Beyond the stars they live and love as yet,
And if in heaven there be red-letter days
This one is crowned with most unusual praise.

The time, the place, to retrospect invite;
But if too long we strain with tear-dimmed sight
Our eyes into the past, we wrong the hour,
The present needs, the future's wondrous power.
Courage and consecration, hand in hand
Have scattered blessings broadcast through the land,
The watchword of the past we make our own.
While all the fields lie yellow in the sun,
To-day is ours; who has a daring deed
To undertake, for life's most urgent need,
Must do it now; whoso would sing a song

129

Must strike the note at once, loud, clear, and strong.
Since first the flaming sword flashed high in air
And Eden closed upon a hapless pair,
No grander time the world has ever known,
No present richer than we call our own.
Oceans may bar and seas divide no more,
Highways of commerce stretch from shore to shore,
And no lone island in the tropic sea
Is foreign to our thought and sympathy;
The earth is wide, and wander where you will,
Some load is there to lift, some void to fill.
"Go you where no one else will go," said she
Who sleeps beneath the ivy peacefully, -
"Do what none else will do, and then
Shall you bear healing to your fellow men."

A word to you whose armor waits your use,
You will allow, since age is garrulous.
Trust not in ease, the confidence you feel
Is in the temper of the untried steel;
Remember that the burnished surface glows
Only though friction which no respite knows.
If sitting at your *alma mater's* feet
You've talked with Aeschylus in accent sweet,
Some soul from you a portion must have gained.
If you would keep the nectar you've obtained,
The world presents its murky atmosphere,
Its clouds for you to lift, its fog to clear.
Be not dismayed at what you find to do,
You need the word and it in turn needs you,
Its cares to lighten, and its loads to lift,
Its blame to suffer and its praise to sift.
These are the tasks that furnish golden keys

To open all your tenderest sympathies.
Where Nature smiles in grandeur and repose
Among the terrors of the Alpine snows,
Where bold Pilatus rears its cloud-capped rock
And frowns upon the heights of Bürgenstock,
And Rigi elevates its summit stern
Above the ancient city of Lucerne,
An old bridge hangs across the rapid Reuss,
Forming an angle, Quaint and marvelous,
And antique pictures 'neath the rafters show
The Dance of Death to those that cross below.
-    A sight to make one pause, and breathe a prayer
Before he treads the dusty thoroughfare. –
Arrow in hand the skeleton appears,
Marking his victims, in all climes and years,
The young, the gay, the aged, and the proud,
For each he has winding sheet or shroud.
But why at feast a skeleton intrude?
Or why should jubilee a ghost include?
Classmates and friends, death's arrows soon or late
Will find us all, we may not hesitate,
Could I but strike one ringing note to-day
Which you, perchance, might hear, and bear away
Into the heated tropics of your lives,
When courage fails and only patience thrives,
That not would be clear, steady, high:
Be brave! Be true! Life's working moments fly.
Morning is transient, dews and freshness cease,
Noontide is crowded, evening brings release.
Beyond the changing lights in which we dwell
Eternal morning breaks, till then – farewell!

Appendix 2
Milton Severance's Historical Sermon,
Sunday, August 16, 1891
preceding the Bennington Monument Dedication August 19.[151]

We have truly a goodly heritage. For some wise and consistent reason God has blessed this great Nation, and given her a name and prestige among the other nations of the earth. All this concentration of wealth and power was begun under Christian light, and has been carried forward by Divine guidance.

The hand of God was over the little band that in 1620 sailed from the harbor of Delft-Haven, under the leadership of such men as Robinson and Brewster, and John Carver, to plant a colony on the barren shoes of a far-off land, that was destined, under God, to change the civilization and government of the world.

There was no *chance* in the whole movement. The Divine plan is seen in its inception, as well as in its progression and final execution. What a sifting God gave the few, who first promised to go, before he sent them forth on their perilous undertaking. The cowardly and base-hearted were sent back to their starting place, and only those who had nerve and toughened sinews wrought into

---

[151] *Dedication of the Bennington Monument and Celebration of the Hundredth Anniversary of he Admission of Vermont as a State*, published by the Centennial Committee, Bennington, 1892, 135-138.

their character and dared a voyage over trackless sea. There was a providence in the stern necessity that drove them out of their father-land, providence in the bribery and treachery that led them to the most inhospitable of the New England shores. It was through just this oppression and hardship that they were trained and imbued with those great and divine principles, which preeminently fitted them to be the founders of Government, and the pioneers of Empire.

But it takes more than *oppression* to make men. Thousands upon thousands were under the yoke of oppression, when the Mayflower and the Speedwell sailed out of port, who never rose to the dignity of men. Europe and Asia are teeming, to-day, with servile minds, only made more servile by the yokes put upon them.

The highest type of character is attained only by men who have just views of God. Those who rule God out of their thoughts and out of their lives, can never be imbued with the highest sense of justice, can never rise to the highest conception of human freedom.

The Puritans were men who made a place for God in their thoughts, in their creeds, and in their lives, and God made a place for them in his universe. They trusted in God and went forward, and the Divine *Logos* led them, with an outstretched hand, out of bondage and over the sea. Those were no ordinary men, that lengthened their cords,[152] and drove their stakes on this continent, and laid the foundations for American civilization and greatness.

They made history, when they acted, and wrote it down, with pens dipped in blood.

---

[152] Phrase is from Isaiah 54:2 and had been used by William Carey in the 18th century to refer to expanding horizons and bringing the Gospel to foreign lands.

To-day is the 114th anniversary of the battle of Bennington. I do not need to refresh your memories with the incidents of this bloody conflict. They are already fresh in all your minds. We have been enjoying the victory for over a century, which our fathers achieved for us, and the record of their valiant deeds is familiar to every household.

The whole country was under a cloud. The reverses of our arms had dispirited the soldiery, and the out-look was depressing to our stout-hearted commanders. Burgoyne with a large force had come in upon us from the North, and had easily triumphed over all opposition, and was pressing his way on, successfully, to form a junction with General Howe at New York. The evacuation of Fort Ticonderoga, was soon followed by disaster at Hubbardton, and Bennington seemed an easy prize to the victor, now halting for supplies at Saratoga. A strong detachment was sent under Colonel Baum to take the provisions, and other military stores, which were held at Bennington. Confident of success, the British general quietly awaited, with his main army at Saratoga, the bringing of the expected supplies. But the distinguished Briton had reckoned for once without his host. He did not know the temper of the steel that he was to encounter. The battle fought was one of the most persistent in the Revolution, as well as one of the most important. It takes rank as one of the seventeen great battles of the world, not because of the numbers engaged, but because of its influence in determining the issues of the war.

When the smoke of the battlefield cleared away, the sun rose with an assured healing in his beams.[153] From the day of the battle of Bennington, our American Freedom was a foregone conclusion. The battle of Saratoga, and the capture of Burgoyne were made

---

[153] Imagery drawn from Malachi 4:2, speaking of the "sun of righteousness."

certain when our sires conquered Colonel Baum, with his following of Indians and Tories. The prestige of the hitherto conquering army was broken, by this one well-directed blow. The spirit of patriotism kindles in our hearts, to-day, as the imagination weaves her fancies around the memories and heroic deeds which our fathers bequeathed to us. We have a right to rejoice and glory in their work. Many of us are their direct descendants. We have heard the story from their own lips.

My one great-grandfather was acting captain in the battle, and two of his sons served under him. We are not ashamed of the ancestral prowess that could rush upon the enemy's guns and wrest them from their gunners; that could charge the enemy within his intrenchments and drive him from them; that could rally from the fatigue and plunder of *one battle* to renew the fight, and win a victory in a second.

These were exceptional men that fought our battles for us, and we do well to commemorate their virtues and deeds of valor.

The nations of the old world put into the most attractive and imperishable form the important facts in their national history. Trajan's Column in Rome, tells the story of his wars, today, after almost twenty centuries, as no page in history is telling it. The Vendome in Paris is lifting up the exploits of Napoleon the First, even after his empire is fallen, to the gaze of admiring beholders. The histories of Florence and Venice are, in their great art galleries, on canvas and in marble, the attractions of the world to-day. England could read her history in monuments, and commemorating buildings, in statuary and painting, on her miles of historic canvas in public halls, and museums, and galleries of art, if the works of her Macaulay, and Knight, and Froude should all be blotted out. Our Nation has not done enough hitherto in this direction. She is too deficient in her historical paintings and historical works of art. She has neglected quite too long these emblematic symbols that are read at a glance of the eye. This battle has lain over a hundred years without its memorial shaft, but at last it has found a fitting monument to bespeak its greatness.

I am not sure but we all ought to be glad of the delay, for in all these years its great conception has been maturing. For well nigh a half century a few earnest and loyal hearts have been watching its inception, and planning for its consummation. At last we have completed the highest single-shaft battle monument in the world.[154] There it stands on yonder hill to tell its grand historic truths to the latest generations. It stands in beauty without a peer. Like the works of the old masters, the Parthenon at Athens or the Cathedral at Pisa, every line is a line of beauty that is wrought into it, and, like every true work of art, it grows upon you the oftener you see it, and the longer you study the graceful proportions.

But we must not think that these great results in conquest and power, have been reached without the aid of the Church. The great formative influence, in molding the character of the people and giving stability and worth, has been the gospel of Jesus Christ.

The town was first settled by a Godly people. Those were no ordinary men who, in 1761, planted the first colony in Bennington. Having by purchase become proprietors of the soil, almost their first work was to make provision for the building of a meeting house, and the next year their church was organized. The whole

---

[154] The Bennington Monument is 306' 4.5" tall. The Washington Monument, the world's tallest obelisk, is 555' 31/8", but it is not a battle monument. The San Jacinto Monument, built in the 1930's, is 567.31', surpassing the Bennington Monument as the world's tallest battle monument. Though taller than the Washington Monument, the San Jacinto Monument is not the world's tallest obelisk, since it is octagonal.

town was deeply interested in all that pertained to the religious welfare of the community. Every man's property was laid under contribution to support the preaching of the gospel. Heir action in town meeting, as evinced by their early records, shows as much care of the church as of their secular interests, even to the decorum to be maintained in the hours of worship. The church touched every interest of the people. Its house of worship was the common property of all, and it was used for all worthy purposes. On week-days the children gathered in an upper room for their education. On the Sabbath their fathers and mothers came with them for worship and spiritual instruction. Here convened the legislature, and after the battle here were confined the prisoners that had surrendered in the contest.

Who can tell the influence of this first church organized within the limits of the State, before any form of government was established over the territory? How much this Commonwealth is indebted to this Institution of God?

It is the mother of seven churches, while it is doubtless the grandmother of twice as many more. What threads of gold these seven churches, and their descendants have wrought into the robe of State! How much real, genuine character they have dyed in the wool, none can tell. They have kept the religious heart beating, and the spiritual fires burning. When the old church has swarmed, the off-shoot has not always been a Congregational hive to abide in. But what matters it, so long as they all hold up Christ as the Saviour of the world? And so long as they love one another, serving the same Master? These churches have helped to rear the men that have given honor to the Nation. The Old Green Mountain State has filled up her quota of men grandly, in every department of industry, of government, and of knowledge, and her churches are what have made her men. We look out upon society, organized on a Christian basis. The church has solved many of the puzzling problems of the past, and it is her mission still to guard the morals of the future. She moulds men, and then men mould the life of the world.

But I must forbear to speak as I would, to-day:

> "I hear the muffled tramp of years,
> Come stealing up the slope of time,
> They bear a train of smiles and tears,
> Of burning hopes and dreams sublime."

The past is seen, the future must be prophesied. But prophecy has its roots in the past. The things we have seen done, as we scan the pages of history, give promise of the things that shall be done. We are progressing toward universal freedom. The mind, as well as the body is breaking the shackles. Social questions and moral questions will eventually find their solution.

In reality the Church of Christ must sound the key-note of all true reforms. For eighteen hundred years she has done it, and to this glorious end she is leading the world to-day.

The Sabbath before our Fathers went forth to battle they gathered in their church edifice to listen to a war sermon from their pastor. They took their cause to the God of Battle, and he heard their cry and gave them the victory. We do not know the preacher's text. We can only imagine that he chose the words of Moses, to be spoke by the priests of ancient Israel, when about to go out to battle: "Hear, O Israel, ye approach this day unto battle against your enemies: let not our heart faint; fear not and do not tremble, neither be ye terrified because of them; for the Lord your God is he that goeth with you, to fight for you against your enemies."

They certainly fought as if under the inspiration of such words, and victory crowned their faith and works, which in true Apostolic fashion went together.

If the walls of the old church could speak to-day, what tales they would tell! But alas, the old edifice has disappeared, and the men that worshiped in it are gone. Their forms have passed silently, one by one, into the old church-yard and lie at rest. But their strong personality is still with us. We feel the presence of an invisible host, whose quiet dignity and matchless grace, whose robust manhood and unflinching courage are the true inspiration of the hour.

As we tread above their graves, and read the quaint inscriptions over which the mosses of a century have grown, we seem to hear, in a kind of solemn under-tone, an exhortation to be faithful to the trusts that encircle us, higher than the Monument that towers above us, more enduring than the everlasting hills is the Church of Christ: "Blessed is the Nation whose God is the Lord, and the people whom he hath chosen for his own inheritance."